COASTAL
GARDENING

COASTAL GARDENING

Julian Slatcher

The Crowood Press

First published in 2005 by
The Crowood Press Ltd
Ramsbury, Marlborough
Wiltshire SN8 2HR

www.crowood.com

British Library Cataloguing-in-Publication Data

A catalogue record for this book is available from the British Library.

ISBN 1 86126 722 3

Dedication
To Fred Roberts, with thanks.

Acknowledgements
No book of this type can be produced in isolation. I have mentioned elsewhere
the inspiration for it and its chief instigators, Tony and Marie Shaw. I would like
to mention here the numerous gardeners whose work features in these pages:
those of Brook Cottage, Alkerton, England; the Botanic Gardens of Wales, near
Carmarthen; the Botanic Gardens of Birmingham, England and of Durban and
Pretoria, South Africa; the Kirkenhoff Gardens, Cape Town, South Africa; the
Holiday Inn, Nazca, Peru; the Mill Gardens, Arequipa, Peru; the municipal
gardeners of Cape Town and Nazca; the garden centres of Burford and
Lechlade, England; Abbottsbury Sub-Tropical Gardens, Dorset, England and
the Royal Horticultural Society gardens at Wisley, England; all deserve thanks,
as do the owners of the many private gardens which are featured here. Also, for
the photographs which I did not take, John Crook and Pru Dunning: thank you
both. And finally, for help in developing the original idea into a publishable
book, The Crowood Press and my father John Slatcher.

Typeset by Servis Filmsetting Ltd, Manchester

Printed and bound in Malaysia by Times Offset (M) Sdn Bhd

Contents

Preface

This book was conceived with the help of two friends from Lancashire, the pub landlords Tony and Marie Shaw.

'Come and see what we've bought', they said one day over a drink. 'Maybe you could help us out with it, and get a book out of it, into the bargain.' So, having agreed a date, I set off north for Scotland. After something over 300 miles of driving, I turned off the main north–south road at Gretna Green and headed west towards the coast. Shortly, I noticed a road sign and read it, I still had nearly 100 miles to go! But it was a pleasant summer day, so I kept going. Finally, at the coast, I passed through Stranraer, then through a small village a few miles further on and out into the thinly populated back lanes. Another couple of miles and, following directions, I turned on to a farm track then passed the farm and kept going. After nearly a mile I reached another house. Now I was getting close. I could see the sea, down to my right. I turned through a field

Thrift and lichens decorate the rocks of the shoreline.

The cottage at Dally Bay.

gate, on to a smaller track, crested the rise and there it was. A bay, maybe 150yd across and, set over to the right, a whitewashed cottage, down by the gently lapping sea. I carried on down, around the front of the cottage. Tony was sitting in his deck chair in the front garden, reading a book; 'Hello', he called through my open car window, 'welcome to Dally Bay.'

Having bought the cottage and experienced the breadth and tameness of the wildlife around it, they had decided that they wanted a wildlife garden. They had enjoyed my previous book, on gardening with wildflowers, and, though there are chapters on seaside gardening in many books and regular fea-

tures in magazines and television programmes, they could not find a book dedicated to the subject. So we decided to plan the one you now hold.

The garden was largely planned on that first visit, starting from little more than an acre or so of rough grass on awkward slopes and angles. Then the work began, and the knowledge used and learned in the process is included here.

With dolphins and seals playing in the sheltered bay, oyster-catchers and nightingales overhead, weasels, voles, hares and badgers, as well as visiting deer, a wildlife garden was the only choice to be made. But in other cases this will not be appropriate. A more formal look might be required. There might be more in the way of shelter or the site might be steeper. It might be an urban garden in a seaside town, perhaps, or even a flat where only window boxes could be used. All these factors and more will be discussed here and many of the plants that can be used will be described and illustrated, although space will inevitably preclude a comprehensive list.

But the main purpose is to provide inspiration, to show what can be done and to prove that anyone, anywhere, with the will to do it, can achieve a beautiful garden, even in the harsh surroundings of a seaside environment. Enjoy your garden and your gardening.

CHAPTER 1

Designing the Garden

The seaside garden has both advantages and disadvantages when compared with sites even just three or four miles inland from the coast. Except in the harshest of winters, coastal gardens are much less prone to frost in temperate climates, and so plants that, inland, would have to be taken in for the winter, here may be left out. A visitor to Scarborough, on the North Sea coast of Yorkshire, for example, will see pelargoniums left out over winter and often still flowering in December. On the other hand, the coastal garden can be much more prone to wind damage than some more sheltered sites and will certainly suffer from salt spray in the air.

This was seen on my first visit to Dally Bay, the garden that inspired this book. After a couple of days parked alongside the cottage, my dark green car was grey with salt. This will be just as harsh on plants as it is on paintwork and therefore the choices of planting in a coastal site need to take this into consideration. Some plants, having evolved in coastal locations, have specific mechanisms for excreting excessive salt from their leaves, leaving them with a crystalline coating that can look exquisite in bright sunshine. Others have evolved different but equally effective ways of coping with the environment.

Wind damage can be eased by the use of shelter, although this should ideally be made up of planting rather than by fences or walls. However attractive the brick or stone of a wall or the wood of a fence, it has no give and so creates as many problems as it solves in a windy site. A solid structure creates eddies in the wind, much as a rock does in a stream. The air behind it is equally buffeted, just less reliably so in terms of direction and strength. Furthermore, the structure itself, holding back all that force, will be prone to eventual failure and thus have to be rebuilt. And, having done that, the plants

Shelter-belt planting is demonstrated by this seaside garden near Cape Town.

A wall is not an ideal windbreak, but where one exists, we might as well make the most of it, as here, where the open door invites the gaze through to the sea beyond and the wall itself provides a home for climbing ivy and a background for the shrubs and perennials of the border. (Photo: John Slatcher)

that were behind it may need to be replaced after having been crushed when the wall or fence fell on them.

Therefore, in general terms, a coastal garden can have more tender species included in it than many

Fences, if really essential, should be made of a material that does not form a solid barrier to the wind.

Dense, lush borders can be achieved on the coast with careful choice of plants.

inland gardens can, but they need to be able to tolerate a salty atmosphere and, where wind is a problem, some form of hedging needs to be incorporated. Allowing for these considerations, a coastal garden can then be designed to suit the needs and desires of the owners, along with the requirements of the site itself.

In the Dally Bay garden the views were a major consideration. They needed to remain unobstructed, as far as possible, limiting the amount of shelter planting that could be used and thus the number of plants that would need it. Also important was the wildlife of the bay; the animals there are largely unused to human activity and so tamer than they would be elsewhere. Normally timid hares and weasels come within a few feet of a person standing quietly in the open. This aspect of the

site needed to be catered for and so a wildlife garden was planned. The ambience aimed for was to be one of harmony with the environment, blending the garden with its surroundings, while giving a feeling of welcome to the people using the site as well. And, with the cottage not occupied all the time, it needed to be a low-maintenance garden, at least for the time being until Tony and Marie could move there permanently. A complex and exacting task, perhaps, but a challenge well worth meeting in a site that was a dream come true for its owners, even before work started.

Sometimes the wide view is more important than shelter or seclusion.

THE PROCESS

There are several good computer garden design programs available, which make the process much easier for those already intimate with modern technology. Programs by Alan Titchmarsh, the late Geoff Hamilton and others are easily available, or you may prefer to use good, old-fashioned pen and paper. Whichever technique you use, the methods are essentially the same.

Start by walking the site with a tape measure and then drawing a scale plan on graph paper, including the north point and the slopes. The existing features, such as the house, drive and oil tank should be included and then all that is to remain unchanged should be gone over with a fine pen, making it permanent. This can then be copied so that you can doodle on it and perhaps make mistakes as you go along. Walking the site again, decide where the important views are, where the sun and the prevailing wind come from, where planting has to remain low and unobtrusive or tall to provide protection. Draw these into the plan.

Then it is time to discuss in detail just what is wanted: any particular plants that are especially favoured, any hard-landscaping features that are required and any other considerations that the family may have. Make notes. First, the hard-landscaping elements are drawn into the plan. Check that these are right. Then the planting can finally be thought about, possibilities listed, some excluded for various reasons, including personal taste and the aspect of the site, and others specifically included for similar reasons.

Whether you use paper or a computer, a similar process to that outlined above needs to be gone through when designing a garden from scratch. In many cases a new owner coming into a home and garden will like some of the elements already in the garden and want to retain them, and will want to change others. If the items to be retained are drawn over with a pen, then others can be pencilled in and erased if they are wrong, without the need to redraw everything. When working on a computer the same effect is achieved by including all the fixed aspects and then saving the design before copying it under another file name and moving on to include new items and planting. The more often the design is saved, the less will have to be reworked if a mistake is found.

Computer design; the programs you can use to do this kind of work include plant lists, each with fully grown sizes for easy placement. What they often do not include is a way of saving your plant list, so it is worthwhile having a notepad by your computer and recording your selections as you go. The program used for this design includes a 3D walk-through facility.

DESIGN ELEMENTS

The first fixed aspect of any garden design is the size and the shape of the plot. This can be emphasized or disguised to some extent, according to the specific needs of the site, by the arrangement of plants, paths and other hard-landscaping elements such as lawn edges, patios, decks and gazebos. A long, narrow plot can be made to look wider, or a wide, shallow one made to look longer, as required. The second fixed aspect is the direction that the

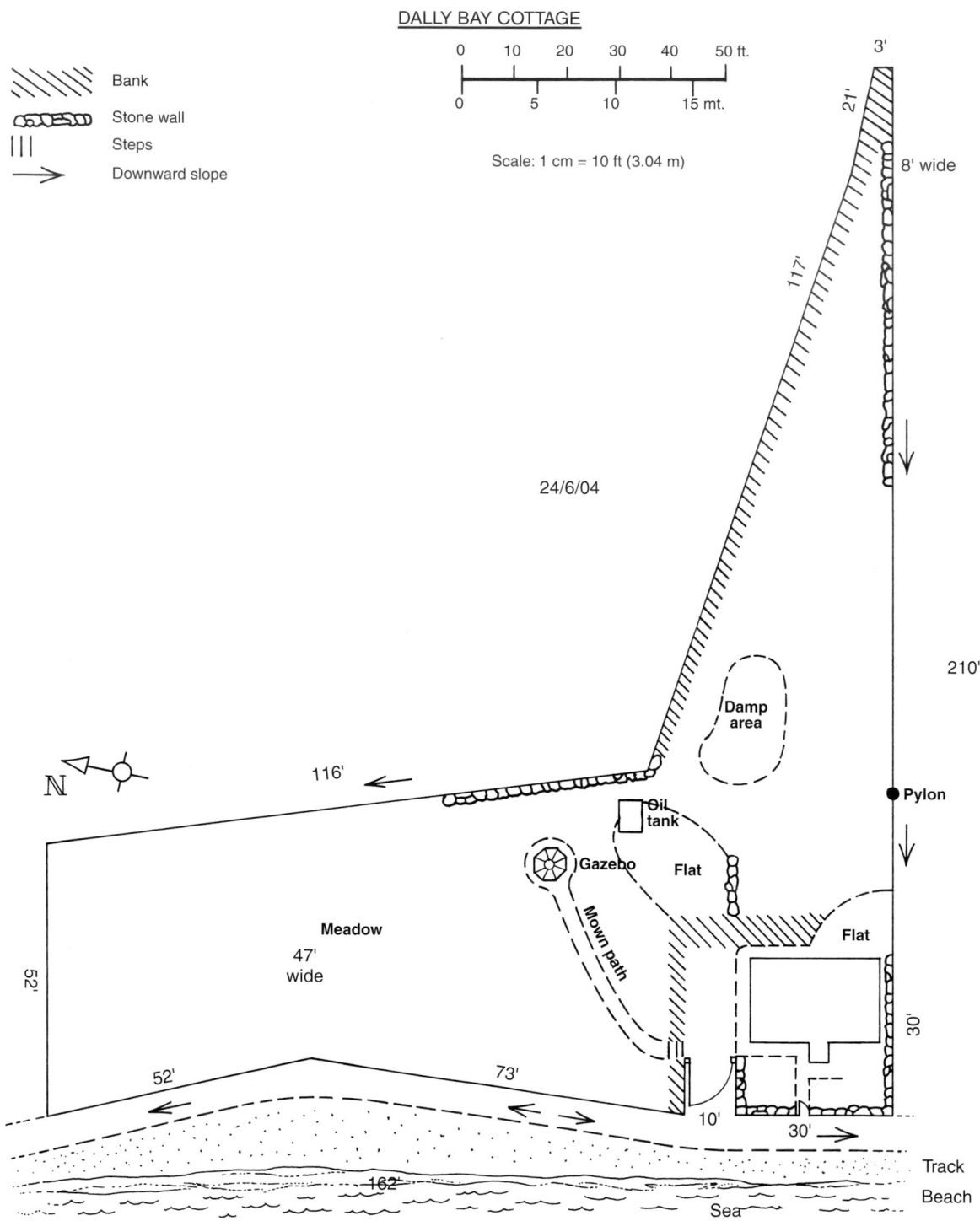

DALLY BAY COTTAGE

Bank

Stone wall

Steps

Downward slope

Scale: 1 cm = 10 ft (3.04 m)

0 10 20 30 40 50 ft.

0 5 10 15 mt.

24/6/04

N

3'

8' wide

21'

117'

210'

Damp area

116'

Pylon

Oil tank

Gazebo   Flat

Meadow
47' wide

Mown path

52'

Flat

30'

52'   73'

10'   30'

162'

Track

Beach

Sea

The first stage of a plan on paper.

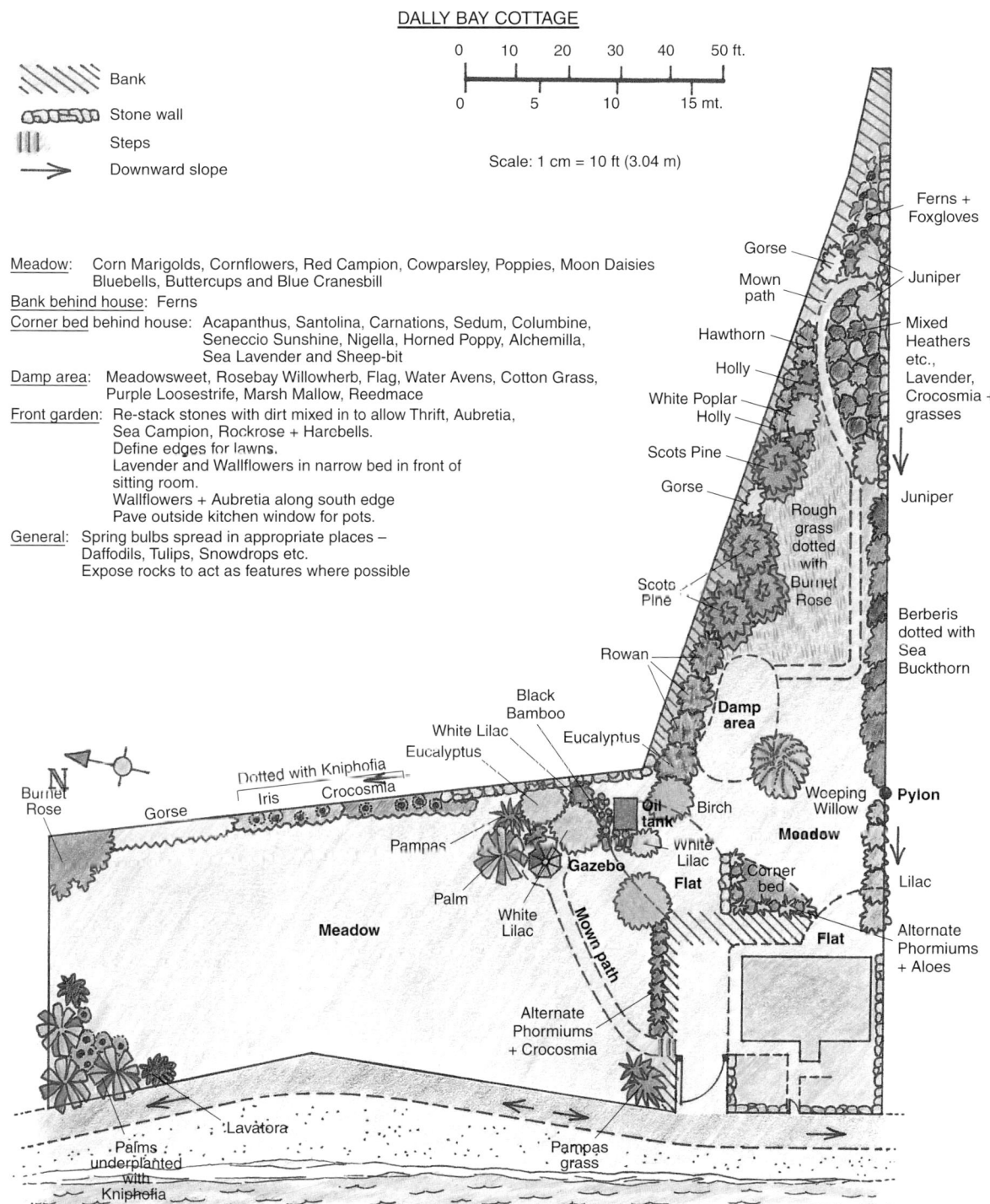

DALLY BAY COTTAGE

0   10   20   30   40   50 ft.

0   5   10   15 mt.

Scale: 1 cm = 10 ft (3.04 m)

Bank
Stone wall
Steps
Downward slope

Meadow: Corn Marigolds, Cornflowers, Red Campion, Cowparsley, Poppies, Moon Daisies
Bluebells, Buttercups and Blue Cranesbill

Bank behind house: Ferns

Corner bed behind house: Acapanthus, Santolina, Carnations, Sedum, Columbine,
Seneccio Sunshine, Nigella, Horned Poppy, Alchemilla,
Sea Lavender and Sheep-bit

Damp area: Meadowsweet, Rosebay Willowherb, Flag, Water Avens, Cotton Grass,
Purple Loosestrife, Marsh Mallow, Reedmace

Front garden: Re-stack stones with dirt mixed in to allow Thrift, Aubretia,
Sea Campion, Rockrose + Harebells.
Define edges for lawns.
Lavender and Wallflowers in narrow bed in front of
sitting room.
Wallflowers + Aubretia along south edge
Pave outside kitchen window for pots.

General: Spring bulbs spread in appropriate places –
Daffodils, Tulips, Snowdrops etc.
Expose rocks to act as features where possible

Ferns + Foxgloves
Gorse
Mown path
Juniper
Hawthorn
Mixed Heathers etc., Lavender, Crocosmia + grasses
Holly
White Poplar
Holly
Scots Pine
Juniper
Gorse
Rough grass dotted with Burnet Rose
Scots Pine
Berberis dotted with Sea Buckthorn
Rowan
Damp area
Black Bamboo
White Lilac
Eucalyptus
Eucalyptus
Dotted with Kniphofia
Iris   Crocosmia
N
Burnet Rose
Gorse
Pampas
Oil tank
Birch
Weeping Willow
Pylon
Meadow
White Lilac
Flat
Corner bed
Lilac
Palm
White Lilac
Gazebo
Mown path
Flat
Alternate Phormiums + Aloes
Meadow
Alternate Phormiums + Crocosmia
Lavatora
Palms underplanted with Kniphofia
Pampas grass

The completed version. Plants are inserted, different colours used to help to define separate areas of the garden and everything is labelled – all in pencil to allow easy alterations.

Even a tiny plot can be made to feel spacious with good use of plants and hard-landscaping elements. Here a gravel 'stream' crosses the garden, emphasizing its width, while large plants give a pleasantly enclosed feeling.

plot faces – a north-facing plot may well be predominantly shady, whereas a south-facing one will catch the sun for most of the day, unless some form of shade is introduced. An east-facing garden will catch the sun in the morning, while a westerly one will be bright in the evening. Areas of shade can be introduced by the use of arbours, gazebos, pergolas and trees. The position of and the shade caused by existing buildings is something that cannot generally be altered, and, if a tree is in an awkward position, then you must check with the local council before chopping it down since to do so might break planning or preservation laws. Sheds and greenhouses can often be moved, but it may require much work to do so, especially if a concrete base

has been used, and fuel tanks may need expert help if they are to be repositioned. Lastly, access gates are often fixed points in a garden. Beyond these considerations, the garden can be designed entirely according to the wishes of its owners.

GARDEN STYLES

Most of the usual garden styles can be used in a seaside garden. You do not have to have a gravel garden or a large rockery just because you are close to the sea. But, having said that, many of the plants normally associated with the cottage garden style

This lush, cottage-style garden is just yards from the beach, on the Kent coast of southern England. Protected by buildings on two sides and sunk below the level of the main road on a third, it is further enclosed with trees, shrubs and trellis.

are generally not suited to a coastal setting, unless plenty of shelter is available. This style of garden would require long-term development, with the early introduction of sheltering bushes and trees, followed only after a few seasons of growth by some of the more vulnerable plant varieties – unless, of course, the site was already sheltered by buildings, perhaps in a more urban setting. However, there is no reason why kitchen gardens, water gardens, formal gardens or even roof or wildlife gardens cannot be made on or near the coast.

Among the first things to consider when designing your new garden are the uses to which you intend to put it. Will you need a shed? A greenhouse? A lawn? A vegetable plot? Compost bins? Is the garden to be a plantsman's plot, largely for the children, for entertaining or just for relaxing, with occasional pottering to keep it all under control?

You may have no control over the size of the plot, but you can control the feel of it and the sense of scale. If you have only a tiny patch you can open up the centre and use small plants and light colours to emphasize the sense of space, or use large, dense planting to hide the boundaries and give an Alice-in-Wonderland sense of size and scale, of being in a small part of something much larger. You may have a large plot in which you need to create divisions in order to produce a sense of intimacy, or you may prefer the large lawn approach, which emphasizes the magnitude of the garden. It may be a long, narrow garden where you need to make it look

A small, intimate seating spot can be created quite simply, whether your garden is large or small. Here shelter-belt hedging and a large pot plant do the job in the romantic style.

wider by the use of curved or angled paths and judicious tall planting. Or, in the opposite case, the shallow depth of a wide garden can be overcome to some extent by similar methods. You may have just a tiny plot at the back of a town house where you want to entertain friends; hard-landscaping will then make up a large part of the design. There is no need to feel obliged to have a lawn if one will not fit into the space you have; in coastal gardens particularly they are high-maintenance features in any case and never look as good as you imagine they will, without much work and a lot of watering.

This tiny plot has no lawns and little space for plants, but the space is fully utilized, with the emphasis kept on the main function of the garden: entertainment.

If there are features beyond the garden that you want to hide, then tall plants, shrubs, trees, trellis and climbers are obvious options; but these can also combine with the use of features within the garden that draw the eye away from the offending items. These methods will also increase the sense of privacy. All these considerations have been taken into account with the design ideas presented here.

SHAPES

The shapes of the several elements of the garden will have a strong effect on its overall feel. Curved lines in the design can give a sense of softness, whereas harsh, straight lines can lend formality, as can brick or tile edging to lawns and other features. Circles have the effect of enlarging the space that they are in. Diagonals also increase the sense of space, leading the eye along them. Lines across the garden emphasize its width, while straight views down its length strengthen that aspect. Blocking the eye with a structure or large plant can encourage the viewer into the garden, making him or her wonder what is beyond the blockage. Allowing someone to see the whole garden at a glance will often cause interest to wane quickly, regardless of what it contains.

While hard, angular shapes will suit a formal, modern feel and round or curved lines will soften a garden, you can counterpoint these effects by the planting, or you can use more than one kind of shape – a round lawn in an angular garden or full,

billowing beds and borders, for example. The combination will dilute the effect and give balance, while the predominance of the round over the angular or vice versa will govern the total effect of the finished garden. The emphasis on one aspect over another will create a coherent style in the garden, without which it would lack impact and meaning, leaving the viewer saying, 'Well, yes, but…'.

Though not large, this plot illustrates the use of all the main garden design elements. Curves and diagonals emphasize its size while the placing of the shed and greenhouse keep some mystery. Lighting aids the use of the garden at night, at the same time being carefully placed to lead the eye around the garden to maximize its size.

USING COLOUR

A predominance of one colour in a garden or border can strongly influence a viewer's mood. Blues and greens tend to be calming, peaceful colours, while white lends purity and light, a fairy-like quality of combined space and intimacy. Yellow is a sunny, happy colour and orange is warm and welcoming. Red is fiery, challenging and dominant, but its diluted variants of pink and purple are more intimate and gentle. Colour can be used to affect the scale of a garden. The cooler colours tend to appear more distant and recessive while the hotter ones tend to dominate and appear closer than they are. In this way a distant point can be made to look closer with a splash of red or a foreshortened view can be lengthened with the use of blues, mauves and whites.

GARDEN FEATURES

With the huge increase in the popularity of gardening over recent years, many garden features can be bought off the peg. Gates, gazebos, water features, arches, fencing, trellis panels, seats, sheds, decks and greenhouses can all be bought from garden centres or DIY stores, shipped home and a minimum of assembly will provide a completed feature. And there are almost endless choices of design available, from rustic to ultra-modern. The trick, when introducing these and other items such as large pots and tubs into your garden, is continuity: matching the styles of all the different items in a coherent manner so that you do not mix cottage with Japanese with modern Western and end up with an aimless jumble. The starting point in the choice of such features is generally the style of the house to which the garden is attached. A 1960s bungalow will look out of place in a cottage garden, just as a Tudor half-timbered cottage will look

Coherent styling of hard-landscaping and planting to match the building they surround give the feel of a colonial house in the tropics, here in Dorset, England.

Even a tiny plot that slopes in two different directions can look good if you are prepared to put in a little effort.

wrong when surrounded by formal Japanese features. Similarly, crazy paving will not look right with an old house or flagstones with a modern brick dwelling. Which is not to say that materials cannot be mixed. In the case of paths, brick can be mixed with stone and tile in the right surroundings, or in garden buildings, metal and glass can mix with wood, if the wood is also modern in look. Soft, rounded lines can be used to ease the harshness of modern materials, or straight, formal ones can lend rigidity to older, softer materials.

Often, the best approach is to begin by studying books and magazines, visiting several garden centres and DIY stores – without any money or credit cards – and getting a general feel for the sort of thing you prefer. Then make the decisions as to what will go together and what is needed before going out to buy specific items in the style that you are looking for. Be it modern lines in traditional materials or in modern ones, an overall, old, maritime look (for which some of the items might come from reclamation yards), a wildlife garden that blends with its rural surroundings, or any other style in between, all things are possible today if you have the time and the money.

A REMINDER

Once you have planned and planted your garden or border, do not discard the plan you first drew up for it. Keep it in a safe place as a reminder of what you put where so that you do not come along later, when plants – especially bulbs – have gone over and died back to ground level or below, and unwittingly dig them up or damage them.

CHAPTER 2

Preparation and Construction

PATIOS

Patios originated as central courtyards in buildings of Roman and Arabic design, the building surrounding an open-air seating area to provide a sheltered retreat from the bustle of the outside world. Nowadays they are rarely enclosed in this manner. The word is now generally used to refer to any reasonably sized, paved area within the garden. Often the patio is at the junction between house and garden, sometimes with patio doors leading out directly on to it. Its use is generally as somewhere to sit out, perhaps to entertain and as a place from which to view the garden. The size of the patio will be dictated by the size of the plot and its planned use. It needs to be big enough for a table seating the expected number of people, with the chairs pushed out so that everyone can sit down at the same time. A 3ft table will need a patio at least 7½ft across (3ft + 3½ft for the chairs when they are out and 1ft for leg room).

It can be constructed from stone, brick, concrete slabs or wooden decking, which will be fixed down on a framework substantial enough to support several people. Gravel may be good for paths and drives but it does not work as a patio surface; the levelling of a table is difficult and chairs are almost impossible to move in and out from the table. This is one part of the garden where materials may be mixed for an attractive effect – crazy paving mixed with brick edging or tile mixed randomly with stone, for instance. The patio can be remote from the house, placed in the best spot for sitting in the evening sun with a drink after a hard day's work. There can be more than one in the garden, to take advantage of the best spots at different times of the day.

The groundwork is vital in the preparation of a

A Mediterranean-style patio garden: almost entirely hard-landscaping, with subtle changes in level to give variety and just a few isolated pockets of simple but dramatic planting, in this case, pelargoniums and a citrus tree.

patio. The earth should be cleared, levelled, raked and then trodden down at a level deep enough to allow for the slabs, the sand base and any cement that you will use to bed the slabs into. The preparation necessary for the construction of any garden feature, including a patio, will be dictated by the type of ground you are working on, especially in a coastal garden, where you may be working in shallow soil on top of rock or deep, sandy soil. The aim is to provide a base that is firm enough for general use without its moving. Therefore, on a deep, sandy soil, construction of any type is much more difficult and footings need to be much deeper and firmer than would otherwise be needed. On such an unstable surface it is advisable to at least treble the depth of the preparatory work.

Patios and driveways both need good groundwork beneath them to stay stable and solid underfoot. Here block paving is laid in a tight pattern. Beneath is a 10cm (4in) layer of compacted hardcore, then a layer of levelled sand, which the blocks are tapped down into before more sand is brushed over them to fill the tiny cracks between.

On a normal soil, a 4cm (2in) layer of sand is laid and levelled. In some cases people will simply lay slabs or paviours on to this and the result will be fine. The sand needs to be compacted and the blocks butted up tightly to each other, then dry sand should be brushed over to fill the fine gaps that will be left between them. However, others recommend the use of a layer of cement under blocks and this is certainly vital if they are to be laid with grout lines between them. Again there are conflicting recommendations: some say use a full layer of cement, with the surface roughened with a trowel to allow bedding in, while others advocate the use of the blob technique, in which four or five trowel-sized blobs of cement are applied under each slab; both methods work. Which you choose depends on your own preferences. In either case, each slab, tile or brick must be levelled with a spirit level and a rubber mallet, both in its own right and

in comparison with its neighbours on all sides, in order to finish with an even surface that will be comfortable and safe to walk on.

The decking has been stained to match the tiles on the edge of the raised bed, while the wall of that bed matches the trellis fence panels to give a coherent colour theme, while the length of the deck is emphasized by the long planks.

Decking should be made of pressure-treated timber and supported on uprights of 10cm (4in) square timber with a framework of 10cm by 5cm timbers fixed to them, the centres 40 to 45cm (16 to 18in) apart. These can be screwed, bolted or nailed with 6in nails, although in all cases they should be pre-drilled to prevent splitting of the timber. The outer framework is put into place and levelled and then the inner beams fixed across that. The support posts, which should be no more than 1.5m (5ft) apart, are then cut off to length. Lastly, the planks of the decking are nailed or screwed in

The different woods used here define the transition between path and patio, while the crossways laying of the path planks lends width and their pale tone brings light into the shady archway.

place with a small gap, usually equal to the thickness of the planks, between them. Modern decking planks are routed with narrow grooves so that the surface does not become dangerously slippery in poor weather. The size and the direction of the decking planks may also be used to good effect in the design of the garden, with narrow planks making the deck look bigger. Planks that lead away from the viewer, rather than across the garden, have the same effect. As an alternative to wooden post supports you can use an existing concrete pad or build small pads of brick or concrete, which are let into the ground about 30cm (1ft), at similar distances from each other as are used for posts. A low-level deck can then be supported on these.

PATHS

Paths may be made of similar materials to patios; but there is a wider choice available in this case: bark mulch, gravel, either of these with slabs set into it as stepping stones and all sorts of materials set into concrete or even simple grass, with or without stepping stones can be used to make paths to get from one point in the garden to another.

The stone risers in this stepped gravel path make it look wider, while its hidden ending leads the eye along it so that both dimensions are made to appear large and spacious.

With the exception of grass paths, which are best suited to relatively light use, any path should be built on a reasonably firm base, much as a patio needs to be. A good layer of sand, compacted clay or ballast will support a path or a patio for years, whereas to put either straight on to the underlying soil will almost inevitably lead to subsidence and unevenness after a while. A layer of plastic sheeting under the construction avoids weeding in the future. Paths may be straight and formal, curved, stepped, solid or made of stepping stones. Their direction in a garden is a vital part of the design, leading the eye around the site. They should therefore be planned carefully before being executed on the ground.

Their width must be adequate to their use. Ideally, they should be wide enough for two people; 1m (3ft) is about right. However, many gardens will not have enough space for this and so narrower paths must be used; 50cm (18in) is common, with any steps at changes of level in the garden perhaps being 60cm (2ft) wide. Path width can be a useful

This slightly raised patio and path, of the same glazed material, lends some formality to this otherwise cottagey garden.

design tool. Narrow paths give the garden a sense of space; paths which narrow as they go away from the viewer make the garden look longer, whereas those that widen as they go away make it look shorter, by perspective. Paths can be made to look wider by the use of low planting at their edges or by a secondary material, such as bricks, used in the same way. They can be softened by close, billowing planting alongside them or formalized by the use of hard edging. It may be useful to lay them around large items in the garden, to lead the eye and the mind on beyond the visible point.

Sometimes paths may be purely functional, as in this case, where a short length of small slabs leads from one part of the garden to another. The foreground shows what will happen to a grass path that is heavily used. In wet weather, this will turn to sticky mud.

ARCHES, ARBOURS, GAZEBOS AND PERGOLAS

Arches may also be of a formal or rustic style and be used simply to allow access from one part of the garden to another or to lead the eye, giving a false

The generous width and the dramatic plant at the top of these steps both helps to foreshorten the view and give more width to a narrow site.

SCENTED SEATS

One of the joys of any garden is the scent of many of the plants we use, especially in a seaside garden where the conditions suit many of the scented plants such as lavender and thyme. A garden seat can be placed in a position where it is surrounded by such plants. Or, with a quantity of soil perhaps left over from the digging of a pond or the levelling of a patch of ground to put a patio or shed on, a seat can be constructed that itself is made up of scented plants. The shape can be formed with bricks, blocks or timber which is then coated with a layer of soil at least 10cm (4in) thick. In this may be planted thymes, chamomile or other scented plants which will tolerate the dryish position and also being occasionally squashed by someone enjoying the scent the plants give off.

Gazebos come in all shapes and sizes.

A line of arches with space between them increases the sense of distance as you look through it.

sense of separation. Indeed, they can be used at the edge of a garden to give a false sense of continuity.

Arbours are generally small, semi-covered seating areas; a patch of privacy in the garden where someone can sit and read or simply think, undisturbed. They are often rustic in design and made up of trellis panels or hedging, perhaps with a tree overhanging. Gazebos can be used for similar purposes, but are generally larger, more out in the open, sometimes more grand in design and take a small table and chairs underneath them or simply a small water feature. They are free-standing, whereas arbours are set into or tightly against a hedge, wall or other boundary. Pergolas can also be free-standing or lean to in design, with one side against a building. They are often used to partly cover a length of pathway or an area of patio and are often of wooden construction and large enough to sit or walk under comfortably. Usually they are covered with climbing plants such as vines, clematis or roses. The famous laburnum walk at Barnsley House in Gloucestershire is a classic example.

Simple, inexpensive, lightweight, metal tube arches can have their bases pushed straight into the ground, going in about 30cm (1ft) to ensure stability. Heavier structures, however, need more groundwork. For wooden arches and pergolas it is possible to use Met-posts or something similar. There are two types: one is driven into the ground, while the other is bolted down to existing slabs or concrete; the bases of the posts are then clamped into them. Where this is not practicable, it is advisable to dig out a hole at least 45cm (18in) deep and a spade-width across for each post. This can then

Sheds, greenhouses and other garden buildings need to be made to look part of the total design. Close planting around their bases helps with this.

be backfilled with a mixture of stiff concrete and rubble in which the posts are embedded. Part-fill each hole with the mixture so that they are all at the same level – this can be checked with a spirit level and some wood – and then place the arch or the pergola into position, ensuring that the uprights are all vertical, and fill around them with more rubble and concrete. A stiff concrete mixture is used so that it will dry more quickly and so that it can be mounded slightly and smoothed around the legs of the structure. This allows water to run off away from the legs and helps to avoid rotting or rusting.

SUMMERHOUSES, SHEDS AND GREENHOUSES

The summerhouse serves a similar purpose to the arbour or a large gazebo in that it is a place to sit in the garden, out of the full force of the sun. There are more designs of summerhouse than there are styles of garden, from small ones that take no more than a couple of chairs to large constructions which can accommodate several people and tables for outdoor parties. These larger ones are often less decorative in design and more like a shed with large windows at the front.

Sheds, like summerhouses, are usually made of wood but may be built of other materials. Often a shed has an electricity supply; it can house the household freezer; it can serve as a workshop or potting shed as well as storage for garden tools and machinery. Style can vary enormously, from the basic, home-made to the very fancy.

Similarly, greenhouse design can vary from the basic to the intricate. Older greenhouses were often built on a brick base, the walls coming up perhaps 2ft, with the greenhouse framework and glass rising above that. Now, for ease of construction, the glass generally goes all the way to the base. But the framework may be of metal or wood and the glass replaced by UV-stable plastic. One thing that is essential to consider when choosing a greenhouse – and the same probably applies to the shed – is that, whatever the size you think you need, it will be too small. Go for at least the next one up.

The siting of a shed generally fits one of two extremes: it will either be out of the way, hidden at the bottom of the garden, or next to the house for convenience. In either case it is best placed on a concrete base or at least a set of brick or block foundation pads. This is not so necessary for a greenhouse, it can be pegged down into the ground or a narrow foundation used and the soil left bare except for a path down the centre. However, the siting of a greenhouse is more important; it is best placed in good light, preferably with a water supply close to hand, and, if tender plants are going to be over-wintered, then some form of heating may well be needed and so power may need to be laid on; but this is not a job for the hobby gardener. An electrician should be employed if that is the chosen power source.

Some gardeners treat the greenhouse simply as a functional building so that it can be hidden away, while others like to place an emphasis on the decorative aspects of the greenhouse. They will fill it with pot plants or alpine benches and it will be a prominent feature in the garden. In either case, access is needed all around the greenhouse to enable the glass to be cleaned.

It may be felt that a greenhouse is not needed at all. A cold frame can then be useful to propagate plants. These serve as mini-greenhouses, simply to provide protection for plants while they grow on from seeds or cuttings. The top of a cold frame is framed glass or transparent plastic, hinged for access, while the walls, usually sloping from about 30cm (1ft) high at the front to 60cm (2ft) at the back, are solid, made of wood or something similar and pegged into the ground.

The weight and structure of a shed or a summerhouse mean that it needs a solid foundation, although in Britain they are legally classed as temporary structures. Even a small shed really needs a cemented slab base, constructed in the same way as a patio would be. Larger buildings need a solid concrete base at least 15cm (6in) thick. This will require about a ton of concrete for an area 4m (12ft) square and will not be a job for a single man with a shovel. The materials can generally be ordered from a builders' merchant and delivered to the site. A mixture of four parts gravel, two parts sharp sand and one part cement with water will produce a good, firm concrete. A mechanized mixer is really needed for a job of this scale, but these can be hired quite cheaply. When laying this amount of concrete a plasticizer should be used in the mixture to delay drying, so that each mixer load will bind with the previous one instead of forming a skin between them, which would make the sections crack away from each other in years to come.

Sheds may come in kit form and are then easy to put together by following the manufacturer's

Even in areas where frost is not a problem, a greenhouse can be useful for its extra warmth early in the season, when you want to germinate seed such as these tagetes and begonias.

instructions. Otherwise, one can be made from whatever materials are to hand – corrugated tin and pallets are often used successfully; the roof may be made of similar materials or be covered in roofing felt, which is nailed down around the edges and along the seams. The edges are then covered with thin battens and the seams coated in a bitumen-based glue/sealant. Further battens are used across the roof at intervals of about 60cm (2ft) to secure the felt to the underlying wooden roof.

GARDEN WALLS

Walls can be used for several purposes other than simply marking the boundaries of a garden. They

GARDEN SAFETY

Most accidents in the home environment occur in the garden. They have three main causes: electricity, water and garden tools. Electricity should be used with care and attention always. For garden lighting there are now low-voltage systems which are far safer than the mains. For tools and for heating in a shed or greenhouse, however, mains electricity is largely unavoidable. Then you should always use a residual current device (RCD) between the power source and the outdoor cable. Cables in permanent outdoor use, such as those taking power from the house to an out-building, should be of a type designed for outdoor use and should be well protected – threaded through a hose-pipe or some other tubing – and checked every year. Water can be as dangerous as electricity; it takes a depth of only 10cm (4in) to drown a person and most garden ponds are far deeper than that. Therefore, if children are regularly present in the garden, some form of protection is vital. A mesh or a grid over the top of the pond may be effective, but is hardly a decorative addition. The same sort of structure placed just a few centimetres beneath the pond surface, however, especially in a solid-lined structure, can be just as effective and completely unobtrusive. Garden tools should simply be easily seen and diligently put up or put away when not in use and all electrical connections checked regularly.

Apart from their structural function, walls can provide an extra place in the garden against which to grow plants.

can support changes in level, with terracing in sloping sites, define the edges of steps in similar situations, separate off different sections of the garden or form raised planting beds. In construction they are generally thought of as being made of brick, stone or concrete blocks of some sort. However, wooden sleepers can be stacked and bolted together to make an attractive, low wall, and, at the simplest, smallest level, planks or metal can form edging to beds or borders, with supporting pegs driven into the ground behind the edging and out of sight.

Walls do not need to be made of a single material. Often an inner, hidden wall of concrete blocks can back a more attractive front face, especially when it is supporting a terrace; and in the front face itself, secondary materials can be used for purely decorative effect – a panel of cobbles can be set into a brick wall, a hole left for viewing through or simply a differently coloured material or layer of different bonding used for contrast.

The secret of building walls in the garden is care and accuracy. A foundation layer of concrete, let into the ground perhaps 30cm (1ft) for a low wall, will level itself to some extent as it dries, although it should be brought to as near to level as possible first with the aid of a spirit level and a length of wood, used to skim the surface. The starting point with this process is to drive in a series of pegs, the tops of which should be at the height of the finished foundation and all level with each other. The concrete can then be levelled to these. Bricklaying takes care and practice in order to become adept at it, but a low wall can be achieved by the beginner. Again, pegs and string are useful with a peg at each end, the string tight and level between them, at the height of one brick and a layer of cement. Bricks are best dampened before being laid since this aids the adhesion of the cement, the consistency of which should be carefully controlled. Do not mix too much at once or it will begin to set before you have used it all. Aim for enough to produce no more than a square metre of walling and make it slightly harsher than the soft mixture used to lay slabs on, with four parts sharp sand, two parts soft sand and one of cement. In the case of walling, it is better to omit the soft sand. The finished cement should be of a consistency that is wet enough to work with easily, but not so wet that it loses its shape when dropped in a small pile from the trowel. Apply a layer of cement on to the foundation and a small amount to the end of the brick that will butt against its predecessor in the wall. If you can get the base layer of cement level, before waving it with the trowel, then the wall will stay

Walls can be integrated smoothly into the garden design by using complementary materials such as the gravel here.

straight, although each brick should be checked for its levelness, both across and along it. After every five or six bricks it is best to check the level along the whole strip also. Tidying up and pointing is done at the end of the construction, with a drier cement mix. For pointing, the tip of a trowel may be used or a specific tool bought for the job. A length of bamboo cane about the thickness of a man's forefinger will work just as well, however, and one will probably be found somewhere in the garden for free.

Where a double-skin wall is being installed the two layers should be tied together at regular intervals with wire wall ties (these can be made from coat hangers if you have enough to spare). In the case of a terracing wall it is best to give it a wide base, narrowing slightly to the top and, where possible, the wall should be sloped slightly backwards to support the weight of soil pushing against it. Drystone walls are also double skinned in construction, the middle often being filled with fine rubble, with the two sections sloping slightly in towards each other. Stones are placed carefully, again with regular tying of the two parts together, so that they balance on each other and knit tightly together. Each space needs to contain a stone that is just right for it, and, if there is not one to hand, then one needs to be shaped with hammer and chisel. The art of drystone walling is in the choice of each stone for its position; in no case is any wobble permissible.

When building any walling time should be taken to do the job thoroughly and well. There is no

Walls do not have to be formal in structure. Local stone, laid to mesh together fairly tightly, can be used, especially if a reasonable backward slope is applied to hold back a change in level almost as you might use a rockery

Instead of capping a drystone wall, you can fill the top 20cm (8in) or so with a mixture of gravel and soil, then plant in this. Small plants can be brought up to a comfortable viewing height in this way.

reason then why your construction should not look good and last for years.

WATER FEATURES

For some people, even a garden on the edge of the sea does not have enough water. They may want to collect fish or simply to enjoy the trickle of a small fountain, for example.

In the heat of summer, especially with the drying salt air of the seaside, a pond can be a welcome source of coolness and moisture.

Ponds may be formal, informal, modern or naturalistic, but all have a few fundamental requirements in common. Whether raised or set into the ground, the edge needs to be level all the way round or some of the liner will show and spoil the effect. Both solid and flexible liners need a layer of sand beneath them, a good 5cm (2in) thick, followed, in the case of a flexible liner, by a material underlay of some sort; old carpet is excellent, if any is available. Flexible liners are easier to work with than the solid plastic or fibre-glass types since more precision is needed when digging and backfilling the hole with the latter. A solid pond needs even support all across the base and the shelves and up the sides too. It is best to dig out a hole at least 30cm (1ft) longer and wider than the liner, smooth the base over with sand and then place the pond liner in it. Start to fill it with water and, as it fills, pack earth and sand around and under it so that no movement is possible once it is full. The edge may then be hidden with paving or planting.

LAWNS

Seaside lawns can tend to look dry, sparse and stringy, unless you happen to live in a river valley. There are ways to avoid this. Watering, where it is legal, is an obvious solution, although it may be expensive and is not environmentally ideal. It is far better to do the correct preparatory work before the lawn is laid. A dry, sandy or stony soil can have topsoil added. This can be bought commercially. If your local garden centre does not sell it, they will most probably know someone who does. Dig in plenty and dig it in well, as if you were making a new vegetable bed. Aim for up to a fifty–fifty mix with the native soil, to a spade depth, if the soil is really poor, less if the soil is of better quality. At the same time, mix in a light dressing of an organic fertilizer and then level the soil and tread it down. If you are trying to restore a poor, existing lawn, spike it well with a garden fork, wiggling the fork at every insertion to open up the holes and then brush in a soil-based compost of the John Innes type. This may be done up to three times a year – in spring, autumn and winter – but it will still take three or four years to have its full effect. Frequent mowing will also improve the lawn's condition and thickness, especially if you water it afterwards too. Watering should be done copiously, but not often, so that it soaks in well, rather than by the little and often method which simply encourages the grass to root shallowly and therefore burn off more quickly when you cannot water it.

A new lawn may be made from seed or turf. Seed is by far the cheaper, but requires more patience. Both methods require the production of a good tilth beforehand. The soil needs to be dug over, weeded, levelled, raked and then trodden down. Using seed means that your lawn will not be ready for use for at least twelve weeks and patchiness may result from visitations by cats or birds. But there is a lawn seed mixture suitable for just about any situation, from sun to shade and from dry to moist. The seed box will tell you how thickly to sow it; but in calculating how much to buy, it is always advisable to overestimate, to allow for the bare patches that will be left by disturbances during germination. Turf, however, gives a usable lawn in just three or four weeks, but is heavier to handle and it must be laid within a day of delivery. Turves should be laid in a staggered pattern, like a brick bonding, in order to prevent long dividing lines from appearing in the finished lawn. They should be butted up tightly to each other; any spaces which are left can be filled with soil or compost and should grow over in time. Turf cannot be laid in dry weather and must be watered if a dry spell occurs within the first few weeks after laying.

A flexible liner is much more forgiving since it simply moulds itself to the shape of the ground beneath it. You simply dig out a hole of the shape you need, but a couple of inches deeper, line it with a layer of sand, then the underlay and finally the liner itself. Fill it with water, smoothing the liner as you do so and then conceal the edge in the same way as for a non-flexible liner. There are two types of flexible pond liner available – plastic and butyl. The butyl one is the longer-lasting and is more flexible but much more expensive. You need to decide on your budget and the size of pond you want and buy accordingly.

A flexible liner allows you to design a pond to your exact requirements.

Raised ponds save much spadework, but need walls to be built up around them instead. They tend to be more formal in style, by the nature of their construction. The walls may be of brick, block or timber. The liner is placed into the construction and filled with water, the edge left to overhang the walls until the capping is applied to the tops of the walls. The liner is then trimmed off so that the edge is hidden. These types of pond are often used for ornamental fish and some digging to deepen the centre can be done if large fish are to be housed comfortably. A pond should be at least 60cm (2ft) deep if fish are to be housed in it. The size of the liner required is easy to calculate: take the length of the pond and add twice the depth, and then the width and again add twice the depth. Add a little for folds and creases and buy according to the figures you have thus arrived at.

BOG GARDENS

There are many attractive plants that enjoy a moist root-run but are not ideally suited for planting in the garden pond. Some of these are suitable for use in a bog garden – a site that is permanently wet or at least damp. This can be created by digging a large hole, as you would for a pond, then lining it with a waterproof membrane which has been repeatedly punctured so that water cannot lie in the bottom and stagnate. The lined hole is then filled in with garden soil and watered heavily before planting up. The planting should be dense or a thick mulch should be used to prevent evaporation. The bog garden must be kept damp throughout the summer with regular top-ups of water.

Regardless of size and shape, a pond needs to be integrated into the garden as a whole. Sympathetic planting around its edges will help to achieve this.

A stone-piered pergola, multi-textured paving and the formal pond leading to the rather grand summer house at the far end illustrate what can be achieved, even in a quite small plot, with time and care.

Where a full-scale pond is not suitable but some kind of water feature is desired, any container that is big enough to hold water can be lined and used. Half-barrels are popular, for example, and readily obtainable. A few plants or a small fountain can be put in and will give a pleasing effect on a patio. Even a couple of small fish can be kept happily in such a restricted home, if a fountain is not used. If a large plant pot is used, the drainage hole in the base can serve as a convenient entrance for the pump cable. The hole is then thoroughly plugged around the cable, the inside lined or waterproofed and the container filled.

On the subject of pond pumps and fountains: these must be installed with safety in mind. The cable needs to be run back to the power source inside a length of hosepipe or rigid tubing and buried underground to keep it out of sight until it reaches the shed or the house from where the power will come. If you are drilling through the house wall to reach the electricity supply, drill at a downward angle, from inside to out, so that the exit damage will be on the outside of the wall and any rainwater will not run into the house through the hole. The cable can be run straight into the shed or the house to a standard plug, or a special,

waterproof, outside socket can be installed on the outside of the wall for the pump to be plugged into. This, however, is a job for an electrician.

FOUNTAINS

Fountains should not be allowed to spray the leaves of water lilies as this will damage the plants and restrict their growth; nor should they be used in a windy site since this will lead to water loss from the pond system. For the same reason, it is not advisable to use a fountain which is higher than one-third of the width of the pond.

With the few exceptions named, all the other jobs described above can be tackled by the careful DIY gardener. Attention to detail, time and patience are essential. We are not all working on a two-day time limit, like some television gardeners. Probably the most important tool in your kit for any construction job in the garden is the spirit level. Use it often and the result of your labours will be as good as anything the professionals could do for you, with the added value of pride in your own work and a boost to your self-confidence.

CHAPTER 3

Planting the Garden

Whether your soil is acid loam, rocky chalk or a mixture of sand and pebbles, the plants you put into it will need a reasonable start in their new location in order to establish themselves. Although many of the plants we are likely to use in a seaside garden have evolved to cope with impoverished conditions, the specimens that you buy from a garden centre, or even plants that you grow from seed in the greenhouse, will have been used to a relatively rich environment. So the soil may well need to be improved before they can be planted out. In really poor soils it can be worthwhile to dig in plenty of organic matter, such as well-rotted manure or loam-based compost, throughout the whole bed before planting. A clay soil will benefit from the introduction of grit too at this stage. Pot-grown and dry-rooted plants will benefit from a good watering before being planted. Soak the roots of a dry-rooted shrub or tree in a bucket of water for an hour or so before planting it. Pots should stand for twenty minutes or so in water before being planted to thoroughly soak the compost and make it easier to remove from the pot with minimal root disturbance.

Pebbles make an attractive and appropriate mulch for a seaside garden. Turn them over and, even in the hottest weather, you will see that they are damp underneath. However close you are to the beach, though, do not take them from there.

PLANTING HOLES

When you plant anything in the garden, especially in a position which is prone to drying out, as many seaside gardens are, it is important to give the plant plenty of room to grow into. As a rough guide, look at the size of hole that you think will suffice for your plant and double it, then mix plenty of organic matter or compost with the soil you are going to backfill around the plant with.

After planting and watering in well – and this means thoroughly puddling the plant in, not just giving it a little moistening – the ground can be mulched with a substantial layer of something like bark chippings, cocoa-pods, gravel or compost to help to keep in the moisture. However, this is not the end of the story, especially in a seaside garden with the predominantly drying winds of most coastal areas. The new plants must be kept watered until they have had a good chance to establish themselves. Regular watering is generally not to be encouraged because the plants become dependent on it: once you start, you cannot stop without losing a large proportion of your plants. However, it is necessary just for long enough to establish them, and again, deep watering is preferable to a light sprinkle since the water soaks down deep and encourages the roots to follow it down. Thereafter they should be allowed to

The slightly more gaudy approach can suit a town-centre garden, surrounded by all the kitsch of the seaside.

CONTAINERS

Containers and hanging baskets can be used in the seaside garden, as in inland ones, but it is even more important here to keep them well watered. Use a good moisture-retentive planting medium and mix in plenty of water-retaining gel granules. Plant densely and, in pots and tubs, use a mulch to prevent evaporation from the soil surface. It is surprising what can be grown in containers, if you are prepared to put the effort into maintaining them. It must be borne in mind, however, that plants in any container are totally dependent on you for food and water. But you can grow anything from herbs, strawberries and tomatoes to climbers such as clematis and even bamboos and trees such as a silver birch in a suitably sized container. One advantage of these, with smaller plants, is that they can be moved easily into a bare patch in the border to provide a temporary fill-in.

fend for themselves. They are, as we said, designed to do so.

CHOICES AND STYLE

The choice of planting will dramatically affect the perceived style of the garden. Even in a strongly structured site, with a great amount of hard-landscaping, the use of soft, billowing planting will soften the overall look and result in a romantic, perhaps cottagey effect. On the other hand, strongly architectural planting can give a hard, formal and sometimes typically coastal

look. The trick is to combine plants in such a way that they complement the hard-landscaping elements of the garden and suit their surroundings, as well as suiting the style you are trying to achieve.

There can be no definitive formula for this. Having decided on the style you want, you then need to examine the gardens around you to see what other people are growing and thus what should grow well in your area. Then visit local garden centres and nurseries to see whether what you find there supports your previous observations. If there is anything that you particularly want, that you cannot find locally, then the Royal Horticultural Society in Britain publishes the *Plant Finder*, which lists all the plants you might want and where to find them for

A bark mulch will help to create a woodland feel, even in a sunny, south-facing garden.

Coherent styling maximizes the impact of any garden. Here the emphasis is on tall planting and grassy foliage.

sale. There are similar publications in other countries: the Society for Growing Australian Plants publishes a smaller work dedicated to their own native species, and in the United States the American Horticultural Society is very helpful. Similarly, the Botanical Society of South Africa will give all the help you might want in that country. These organizations are there to promote horticulture and will readily do all they can, particularly for their members or prospective members.

It is often said that the taller plants should go to the back of a border, tapering down to low-growing specimens at the front, and, indeed, this is a method that shows off all the plants to the best effect. However, it is also true that there should be some mystery in a garden. You should not be able to see the whole at once, or it loses interest quickly. Therefore some taller plants at the front of a border may be helpful from a design point of view. These can then be interspersed with some choice miniatures.

If you are designing the garden from scratch you will have to decide where to put the planting beds and borders before you can go on to fill them. They should be easily accessible for maintenance as well as for admiration. A large border can benefit from having a small path along the back of it, for instance. The shapes of the borders should match the general style of the garden. Softly curving bor-

ders will not suit a formal layout, whereas straight lines will not suit a cottage style, to take the extremes. Triangular beds can tuck neatly into corners at the edge of a patio, for instance, and be viewed from either side, like an island bed in the lawn. Ponds, if you choose to have one, benefit from being planted around at least some of the sides, while leaving at least one side open for access, again for maintenance as well as for the close viewing of the specimens contained there.

No border, unless it is filled seasonally with bedding plants, can succeed all year with just

Carefully mixing tall plants with shorter ones can add impact to both. This border is also narrow enough for easy maintenance.

Photographed here in spring, this tiny garden maintains colour and interest all year by the careful selection of both shrubs and filler plants such as bulbs and annuals.

annuals and herbaceous perennials. It needs a permanent structure. Shrubs, evergreens and decorative grasses will be the mainstays of this element of the garden, which is why they are generally chosen and planted first so that the result will look attractive with just those. Then the perennials and the annuals are used to fill in around them and add seasonal colour and interest.

The final sizes of the plants you choose will determine the distance that they should be planted apart and therefore the number of them that you need. Check these carefully and plant accordingly. It will look gappy to start with, but in a season or two it will fill out and, in the meantime, you can use annuals to fill the gaps.

In choosing plants for your borders it should be borne in mind that they need to vary in leaf colour and texture as well as in size and flower colour. A

Interest is maintained here with hardly a flower in sight. Leaf shape, colour and textural differences do all the work for much of the year, with occasional accents from flowers.

Repetition of both leaf form and flower colour gives this border a coherent theme.

border, or part of a border, will look like a feature-less mess if all the plants in it are of a similar colour and texture, regardless of their flower colour and size. You should aim for contrasts in texture, putting, for example, the feathery, light green foliage of cosmos in front of the rich, dark, leathery leaves of a fatsia or around the spiky form of a cordyline. Leaf colour may also be used to add interest and contrast, mixing dark with light, brown with variegated, glaucous (bluish) with yellow or silver with black. The degree of contrast can be con-trolled for subtle or dramatic effect. Having achieved that, flower colour can then be as varied or similar as you wish. There are famous, single-colour borders such as the white border at Sissinghurst and the red one at Hidcote. These succeed because the plants bearing the flowers are suffi-ciently different to maintain interest. You can go for a planting scheme that provides flowers of harmonious or clashing colour range. Nature mixes all colours; you can too, if you wish.

Repetition is another useful trick. Using a partic-ular plant in several places through the garden gives continuity and can tie together different areas of it. Where one bed might be predominantly blues and whites, while another is reds and yellows, for exam-ple, the use of a particular shrub in both or different colours of the same plant – white dahlias in one

border and red in another, perhaps – can tie the two together and make them appear as two parts of a whole instead of as two totally unrelated areas.

EDIBLE ORNAMENTALS

Many garden flowers are edible – pot marigolds and nasturtiums are well-known examples. But many herbs, vegetables and salad crops are also decorative enough to be included in even a quite formal flower garden. Strawberries have both their flowers and later their fruit to look appealing over a long period. Some dwarf and trailing tomatoes have been bred specifi-cally for use in tubs or hanging baskets. Lettuces, especially the cut-and-come-again types, can look very ornamental among the more usual inhabitants of the flower border.

POSITIONING PLANTS ACCORDING TO THEIR NEEDS

While it is true that all the plants described here – and many more besides, of course – are suited to a coastal environment, there is still variation in pref-erence within that description. Some like shade, some like sun; some like damp conditions while others prefer dry; some like acid soil and some alka-line. These points need to be borne in mind when

This south Devon garden is a testament to what is possible. Turning to the right would reveal a view of the sea through a shelter-belt of trees and shrubs.

choosing and positioning your plants and when deciding on plant combinations. It is no use thinking that a clematis will look good climbing through a rhododendron, because one likes acid soil and the other a neutral or alkaline one. You need to check the conditions of your garden. Buy and use a soil pH testing kit since soil acidity can vary from one part of a garden to another. Check too the overall dryness of the soil. In the Dally Bay garden which inspired this book, it was noted on a first inspection that there was a damp area in the middle of the garden, behind the house. This was in June and so it was a reasonable assumption that it would remain damp all year and so could be used as such. It is always a good idea to use the prevailing conditions of your site rather than to try to fight against them. In the case of a damp patch, it could be drained, but it would involve much work, and so you might

There are so many plants to choose from that you can create whatever mood you want to, almost regardless of your garden conditions. Here a light, airy feel has been produced despite the damp conditions of this stream valley.

as well use it, unless it is in completely the wrong place. Heavy clay can have organic matter and grit dug into it, but it will take you years to produce a good loam, if it is ever possible. Dry, sandy soil can have loam and manure added to it, but the same is true, and stony soil will forever be stony, no matter what you do since every time you dig the ground over, you will lift more stones, however many you may remove. Soil acidity may be altered artificially with chemical additives, peat or lime. But it is far easier and more effective in the long term simply to choose plants that will enjoy the conditions you have, rather than begin a running battle to keep something alive that really is not suitable for your site.

This and the expanding public knowledge of and concern with conservation issues have contributed to the current trend towards using native plants in the garden – plants which have evolved in a particular country or even an area of it, where you are gardening. Indeed, this work is part of that trend, with its emphasis on using plants which will thrive in a coastal environment.

However, if there is a plant that you feel that you simply must have but one that does not suit the conditions of your garden, there are two ways of tackling the matter, apart from simply not buying it. The first is to look at the ultimate size of the plant and dig a planting hole that will be more than big enough to accommodate the roots when it has grown to full size. You then backfill around the plant with a planting mixture that will suit its growth. The second method is to use a container; any plant, as we have noted, from the smallest rockery specimen to a full-sized tree can be grown in a container, if you are prepared for the work it will entail. Simply pick a suitably sized container and fill around the plant with a suitable planting mixture, with plenty of organic matter in it, then keep it well watered and regularly fed. Neither of these methods is perfect, but they will allow you to have whatever plants you want in your garden without restricting you to those that would naturally survive there.

There are thousands of plants to choose from and more than enough to satisfy even the most demanding gardener, whatever your situation. Check the labels on plants before you buy them, to

---

UNUSUAL PLANTERS

Interest can be added to your garden by the choice of a few, select, unusual features, some of which may be used as impromptu planters. Items picked up on the beach can often be used in this way, such as a sufficiently large piece of driftwood placed at the side of a patio or the front of a border and perhaps planted up with small rockery plants such as sempervivums or saxifrages.

---

see what soil conditions they enjoy, and, if you have them, fine. If not, do not buy unless you are prepared to work to keep the specimen alive.

PLANTING

Having said all this, the planting stage is the time at which you should improve the soil a little, in order to give the plant a fighting chance, whatever the conditions it prefers. A large planting hole is always preferable to one that just fits the pot that the plant is coming out of. This hole can then be backfilled around the new plant with a mixture of combined soil, compost and a little fertilizer. It can be helpful too on particularly dry ground to incorporate a little water-retaining gel in the planting mixture, especially if the plant does not have a naturally large or deep root system.

Plants should be firmed in well, destroying any air pockets and forming a good contact between the root ball and the surrounding soil. It is rarely necessary to tread the plant in with a boot, unless the soil has a tendency to form sticky lumps, when you should really not be planting anyway. Use the fingertips or knuckles to push the soil in tightly around the plant and leave the surface slightly dished around it, so that water will collect around the plant instead of running away from it. Some of the plants commonly used in seaside gardens, however, will rot off if their necks – the junctions between stem and root system – are allowed to sit in wet soil in winter. These include many of the rock garden alpines, such as the lewisias and similar rosette-shaped succulents. They are best planted slightly higher than the soil surface, then mulched with grit or gravel; alternatively, they can be planted on a slope, so that their crowns do not lie level and water can run away from them instead of collecting in or around them.

The Crown Imperial, a stately plant up to 1m (3ft) tall in flower, is one of the few exceptions to the rule of planting bulbs at roughly three times their size in depth. Instead, they need to go in as deep as 20cm (8in) or they may not flower.

In a garden that goes right down to the beach, as here, some form of shelter from high tides is needed. Here, large stones have been brought in. Planting pockets can be created among these with a mix of gravel and soil, in which mat-forming plants such as aubretia, diascias and mesembryanthemums will take freely and can be accompanied by irises, grasses and small shrubs like the santolina. In this way the sea can be brought visually right into the garden. (Photo: John Crook)

Even these succulents and cacti can survive a British winter on the coast, if planted correctly. A large hole and plenty of grit in the planting mixture and a grit mulch to keep their necks free of excessive moisture will see them through even a covering of snow.

Clematis, on the other hand, is best planted deep, with the crown at least 10cm (4in) below the soil surface. This encourages more basal shoots and increases the chances of surviving clematis wilt, should it strike. Roses should also be planted with the crown a few centimetres below the soil surface to encourage basal shooting. Bulbs should be planted at a depth of about two and a half times their own height; so a 5cm (2in)-tall bulb should go into a hole 15 to 20cm (6 to 8in) deep. It is often beneficial, in heavier soils, to add a little sand to the soil under and around bulbs, to assist drainage and prevent their rotting over winter. There are exceptions to these general rules. The nerines, for instance, like to be at the surface of the soil so that the bulb tips are baked in the sun through the summer months.

Some gardeners insist on scratching over the surface of the root ball of plants in order to encourage

HERBS

Most herbs enjoy the dry, sunny conditions that tend to prevail in a seaside garden and they can be used in a number of ways. Some may be grown in the flower borders, others can be successfully cultivated in pots, tubs or hanging baskets. Some of the more vigorous herbs, such as mint, are best grown in a container, where their tendency to spread can be controlled. For purely culinary use, as well as being a decorative method of growing, some people use a herb wheel: a circular patch of earth is dug over, grit and compost may be added if necessary. Then bricks are used, on a bed of cement, to form an edging to the circle and to form divisions across it like the spokes of a wheel. A central hub of brick or concrete may be used for standing a large pot or statue on. Each sector is then planted with a different herb so that they do not mix and are easily harvested.

STAKING

Many taller or lax-stemmed plants can have their appearance improved greatly, especially in an exposed site where wind might damage them, by the careful use of staking. This can take several forms, from the twin rows or wigwams of tall bamboo canes often used for runner beans and sweet peas, to the ring of interlocked link-stakes which can keep a geranium or peony upright in the border. The trick with staking in the border is to make it as unobtrusive as possible. This means staking early, before the plant needs it. It will mean that the stakes are obvious for two or three weeks before the plant grows up through them, but once they achieve full size their stems and leaves will hide the stakes within their bulk. A note of caution with regard to safety is important here: if you use narrow-topped stakes, such as bamboo canes, cap them with something relatively broad such as an empty film pot or one of the decorative cane-tops now available. It avoids the possibility of putting your eye out when leaning into the border to perform some maintenance task later in the season.

the roots to spread out into the surrounding soil, while others do not. It is a matter of choice to some extent, but a particularly root-bound plant, where the roots are growing around the inner surface of the pot will benefit from having them teased out, so breaking this habit.

In an exposed, windy site, larger plants, such as trees and shrubs, should be planted when they are as small as possible. This allows the plant to establish a good root system before the top growth gets big enough to suffer buffeting by the wind. It does not allow for instant, television-makeover gardening, but it does give the plant a much better chance of survival. Where a larger specimen is all that is available, staking is essential. The stake should be driven in at an angle of about 45 degrees, close to the stem or trunk and low down, perhaps 30cm (1ft) above the root ball. Then the stake is tied to the tree or shrub with a tie that is suitably big enough and crossing it between the stake and the plant to cushion the bark. Stake ties should be checked regularly and not allowed to become tight on the plant thereby affecting its growth.

It is wise to know a little about plants before you handle them. These euphorbias, if damaged, exude a milky sap that can irritate the skin, so they are best handled with gloves.

TRANSPLANTING

In any garden redesign project, there may be some plants that need to be saved from the old layout. If they need to be moved, then it is best to do so in spring or autumn, when growth is slow. If this is not practicable, however, there are ways to ensure the survival of the plant, despite the non-ideal conditions. Herbaceous perennials can simply be dug up with plenty of earth around the roots, to minimize disturbance, and replanted and watered in well, in the same way as you would settle a pot-grown plant into its new home. In the case of shrubs, pruning will help. Again, plenty of root-ball is desirable, to minimize root disturbance. You should dig around the plant, starting at about 30cm (1ft) outside the area covered by the top growth and work inward until you begin to see signs of root growth, then stop and work under the plant. Any major roots growing beyond this main root ball can be severed. In addition to this, if the top-growth is trimmed back by about one-third, then the loss of water by transpiration is cut down and the roots are given a chance to become established in the new site without undue strain being put on their water-gathering capacity. Checking the growing instructions on the particular plant will give you an idea of the preferred method of pruning, and, if this allows more than a third to be taken off, then do so.

Where a plant cannot be dug up and immediately replanted owing to the timescale involved in the redesign project, then its roots should be wrapped and kept damp. The plant should then be stored in a shady spot until it can be replanted at the first opportunity. Where it is feasible, the temporary potting of the specimen is a useful method of storage.

Whether using old or new plants, it is said that

A simple combination of common plants can provide great impact if done well.

A LOW-MAINTENANCE SHRUB BORDER

A method which has been used successfully for the production of a weed-free shrub border is first to dig over the ground and remove as many of the weeds as possible, then cover it with a sheet of black plastic. This is buried around the edges and crosses are cut in it through which to plant shrubs or evergreen perennials. The triangular corners of the cut plastic are buried in the sides of the planting holes and the sheeting is then covered with a thick mulch of bark, grit, cocoa shells or something similar. To prevent this from becoming a large cat-litter, the mulch can be sprinkled with rose-clippings, just thickly enough to discourage the offenders from crossing the bed.

variety is the spice of life. However, it is also said that numbers count. Plant several specimens of a few types of plant for impact. All the major gardens prove this point. A bold clump of each plant will stand out and make a statement, whereas many individuals will clamour against each other for attention and none will be clearly seen. This may go against the grain for a keen gardener with a plot of limited size – you want to cram in as much as possible, to enjoy as many plants as you can fit into your limited space. But stand back, close your eyes and imagine the finished garden: imagine one agapanthus among a mixed border, then imagine a bunch of them in that border, next to a bunch of crocosmia. Back that with a dark-leaved shrub and you have impact. Less is more.

CHAPTER 4

Annuals

We have divided the myriad types of plant that can be used in the garden into annuals, perennials (including biennials and bulbs), shrubs, trees and climbers because each of these categories has its own uses, advantages and disadvantages.

Annuals are the short-term show-stoppers of the garden. They are what gardeners use for instant impact and when they want a bright, colourful display that can be changed from season to season. The disadvantage with this approach is that it is labour-intensive. This is not the lazy person's gardening technique. However, although perennials can give just as bright a display, there is nothing like the short-term, use-them-and-dump-them approach of using annuals if you want to have the garden giving the maximum impact all year. Having said that, several of the plants which parks departments across the world use in this way are, in fact, perennials (some hardy, some not) and so they are included in that section. Examples of these include the pansies, primulas, pelargoniums, lobelia and the bulbs.

The purpose of all flowers is the propagation of the plant by the production of seed. Annuals, by definition, live for only one year and so must grow to size, flower, set seed and allow it to disperse all within that one year. Hence they grow fast and flower quickly and intensely. Most will be big enough to plant out within six weeks or less from sowing as seed. They will then flower shortly after that. From this you would expect a short display of flower, followed by the quick production of seed and then fading. Left to themselves, the wild types of annual will often do just this, but we have two things in our favour as gardeners. The first is that the plant is determined to produce seed and will keep flowering until it can do so. Therefore, if you keep cutting the flowers off before they can set seed, the plant will keep producing more flowers.

A classic annual bedding plant, the French Marigold, Tagetes patula, will flower for many weeks, especially if regularly dead-headed.

And the second is breeding – the original genetic engineering. Plants have been bred for the garden for thousands of years. Many have been bred specifically for a longer flowering season. Others have been bred to be sterile and unable to produce seed; of itself this lengthens the flowering period.

Another advantage of annuals for the seaside gardener, especially, is that their relatively short growing season means that they tend to stay fairly small and have relatively small leaves and flowers, although they generally have many of the latter. There are, of course, exceptions to this, including the few annual climbers, which can put on several metres of growth in a season and sometimes have quite large leaves; the hop is an example. A further advantage of these for the seaside gardener is that they die off in winter and so avoid damage by bad weather, unlike their perennial cousins, with which they are grouped in this book (*see* Chapter 7).

Combining these factors, then, we can have annuals in flower for many months. Mixing these with bulbs and some of the perennials which are used in the same way as annuals, such as the primulas and pansies, we can have flowers in the garden practically all year, especially in milder, coastal regions.

Callendula officinale *Pot marigold.*

Callendula officinale Pot marigold

A hardy plant with mid-green, slightly hairy foliage and prolific, bright orange flowers produced over many months, especially if seed is planted the previous autumn. Very easy to grow and was used as a herb for salads in previous centuries. The flowers are edible. Will flower in about ten weeks from a spring sowing. Benefits from having the tips pinched out to encourage bushiness. Varieties are available which grow to between 20cm (8in) and almost 1m (3ft) tall; flower colours from creamy yellow through orange to dark red. Will tolerate sun or shade and any good garden soil. Best sown from seed where the plants are to flower. Flowers from June to October.

Centaurea cyanus *Cornflower.*

Centaurea cyanus Cornflower

Once common in British farmland, this plant has become rare in the wild, but conversely has thrived in gardens, where it has been bred to produce double flowers in colours from white through pastel pink and blue to dark red as well as the original dark blue. Wiry stems hold sprays of flowers up above thin, greyish-green leaves. Can benefit from low staking or growing among other plants, which will lend it support. Regular dead-heading will prolong flowering through the summer and early autumn. Varieties are available which grow to anything between 30cm (1ft) and 1m (3ft) tall. Grows in sun or partial shade in any well-drained garden soil. Best sown from seed where it is to flower. Sow in autumn or spring. A good cut flower. Flowers from June to September.

Chrysanthemum segetum *Corn marigold.*

Chrysanthemum segetum **Corn marigold**

As the name suggests, another formerly common flower of the fields, now much less so. It has never attained the garden popularity of the cornflower since it has plenty of relatives which give more showy displays, often on smaller plants. There are many members of the chrysanthemum family in cultivation, from annuals through perennials to sub-shrubs and from 25cm (10in) to between 1.3 and 1.7m (4 to 5ft) in height. All have the characteristic daisy flowers and lobed leaves which are inclined to droop when water is short; but few are as hardy as this native of Britain and western Europe. All benefit from some shelter from strong, drying winds. Corn marigold flowers are about 4cm (1½in) across and bright yellow. It gives maximum impact when planted in a group. Tolerates any good garden soil, in sun or partial shade. Likes the support of growing among other plants. May be pinched out when young to encourage branching. Sow where it is to flower. Flowers from June to October.

Clarkia elegans *Clarkia.*

Clarkia elegans **Clarkia**

Easy to grow, hardy annual which comes in single or double varieties, with flower colours from white through salmon to purple, above slightly greyish-green foliage. Formerly known as godetia, double ones look like tiny hollyhocks. Flowers are borne in upright spikes from 30 to 60cm (1 to 2ft) tall. Will benefit from some support in exposed situations. Prefers a light or medium soil structure and slight acidity in full sun. Does not tolerate root distur-

bance and so should be sown where it is to flower, in spring. A good cut flower. Flowers from July to October.

Cleome spinosa *Spider flower.*

Cleome spinosa **Spider flower**

This large, bushy plant looks very exotic, with its long stamens and pink or white scented flowers above narrow, lance-shaped, mid-green leaves. Young plants are attractive to greenfly. Not fully hardy where frost is a problem and so should be sown indoors in trays if this is the case. Sow seed in autumn or early spring, pinch out tips when 5 to 8cm (2 to 3in) high and plant out when the risk of frost is past. This is less of a problem in many coastal gardens, where you should be able to sow the seed where it is to grow in spring. Prefers a fertile soil with good drainage and full sun. Spectacular when planted in a group, but equally outstanding as a dot plant in a bedding scheme. Grows to 1 to 1.3m (3 to 4ft). Flowers from July to September.

Cosmos bipinnatus *Cosmos.*

Cosmos bipinnatus Cosmos

The feathery, fennel-like, mid-green foliage of this plant is almost as attractive as its wide, daisy flowers, which come in colours ranging from white through pastel pink to deep red. Mixtures or single colours of this popular and easily grown plant are readily available from seed merchants and garden centres. It is related to the orange-flowered perennial *Cosmos sulphureus* and the almost black-flowered *Cosmos atrosanguineus* or chocolate cosmos. All come from Mexico and are not fully hardy but will do well in most coastal gardens, especially if continuity is ensured by taking cuttings of the perennial varieties. The annual *bipinnatus* should be sown from seed in early spring, in trays or in the ground if in a frost-free area. Well-drained soil in full sun is preferred. Flowering is profuse and extended by dead-heading from July to October on plants which can reach almost 1m (3ft) in height unless a dwarf form is grown.

Escholzia California poppy

The California poppy is widely grown for its profuse display of flowers above greyish foliage on plants that reach only around 20cm (8in) in height. Modern hybrids can give flowers from white through to deep red, as well as the usual bright orange. These plants enjoy full sun and well-drained soil without too much nutrient content.

Escholzia *California poppy.*

They flower freely from June to September and will self-sow in soil that they are suited to. However, these seedlings may be disappointing and so it is best to pull them up and sow fresh seed yourself in autumn, where they are to grow, since they dislike root disturbance.

Gazania krebsiana *Gazania.*

Gazania krebsiana Gazania

One of the profusion of plants to come out of South Africa to decorate the gardens of the world, the Gazania is a showy annual whose flowers, in orange and burgundy tones, are seen at their best in full sun, in well-drained soil. The low plants, up to 40cm (16in) in height, display their flowers on short stalks from June through to October, but the flowers open only in the sun; in dull weather they stay stubbornly closed. However, a massed display on a bright day is a spectacular sight, especially when it is mixed with some of the other daisies such as osteospermum and marguerites, in contrasting colours. Ursinias and arctosis, as well as dimorphotheca are broadly similar in appearance and equally useful in the garden. They grow to 18 to 40cm (7 to 16in) and are well-suited to the seaside environment. Sow seed in trays in spring and plant out into their flowering positions in early summer.

Helianthus annuus *Sunflower.*

Helianthus annuus Sunflower

All children know sunflowers as the easily grown giants with yellow-rimmed, plate-sized flowers high at the tops of sturdy stems that remind one of old nursery rhymes. However, there are more sensibly sized examples for the garden border, growing to anything from 60cm to 1.5m (2 to 5ft). They all prefer a sunny position in any good garden soil. Seeds may be sown where they are to flower, 2 or 3cm (1in) deep in spring, for flowering from July to September. Even the largest varieties look best planted in clumps, rather than singly, as tends to happen with the giants. Then a true impact can be achieved, whatever the scale of the plant or its situation.

Ipomoea tricolor Morning glory

Like clematis, this scrambling twiner can be grown as a climber on a trellis or weaving through a border. The large, teardrop leaves are not plentiful and so the morning glory is not the plant for forming an effective screen, but it is attractive in itself, quite apart from the spectacular blue trumpet flowers which, though individually short-lived, are borne in profusion from July to September on plants which grow up to 2 to 4m (6 to 12ft). They prefer full sun,

Ipomoea tricolor *Morning glory.*

but require some shelter from harsh winds in any good garden soil. The seed should be soaked for twelve to twenty-four hours before being sown in pots in spring, for planting out when the plants are large enough to handle comfortably.

Lavatera trimestris *Annual lavatera.*

Lavatera trimestris **Annual lavatera**

The pink or white flowers of this bushy plant provide a good show of colour in sun or partial shade, regardless of the soil type. The flowers are long-lasting and up to 8 to 10cm (3 to 4in) across, on plants that can grow up to 0.7 to 1.2m (2 to 4ft) tall, depending on the variety chosen, growing fast enough to be in flower by July from seed sown in March, although they can be sown in autumn and over-wintered where they are to flower. Excellent for the middle or back of a border and they will self-sow freely.

Lotus berthelotii *Coral flower.*

Lobelia erinus *Bedding lobelia.*

Lobelia erinus **Bedding lobelia**

There are many species among the lobelia family, from the small bedding and hanging-basket types through the spectacular, scarlet, perennial species that is so popular with water gardeners, to huge plants that thrive on the sides of Mount Kilimanjaro in Kenya, where they suffer daily temperature variations of -4 to $+30\,^{\circ}\mathrm{C}$ or more. The bedding varieties are not as hardy as that, but they are far more useful in the garden; indeed, they are among the most widely grown plants in the world, as edging for beds and borders. They come in a variety of colours and flower from June to September, on plants just 10 to 15cm (4 to 6in) high. They prefer rich, moist soil, but will tolerate most conditions, in sun or partial shade. Although mature plants can survive a light frost, seed and seedlings are tender and so should not be planted outside until any risk of frost is past. They are best sown in trays and potted on in small clumps to maximize impact when they are mature.

Lotus berthelotii **Coral flower**

Like the Lobelia, this is, in fact, a perennial, but is used in the garden as an annual. It is a trailing sub-shrub, related to the British native bird's-foot trefoil, although much more spectacular in appearance, with its grey leaves setting off the flame-like, orange flowers. It needs full sun and prefers well-drained soil. Seed can be sown in spring or autumn for flowering from July to September. Cuttings may be taken from non-flowering shoots and rooted in well-drained compost. A favourite for hanging baskets and the edges of tubs, especially in sunny locations.

Lunnaria annua *Honesty.*

Lunnaria annua **Honesty**

This hardy plant will grow in sun or shade, although it prefers partial shade. It can be sown from seed in late summer or autumn, the tips of the plants being pinched out when they are a finger-length high to promote bushiness. The pink or white flowers are held high on thin stems up to 1m (3ft) tall above the broad leaves, from April to July and followed by the characteristic, flat, round seed pods which turn semi-transparent as they ripen and look marvellous through autumn and winter, if left on the plants. Although the name implies that this plant is an annual, it is in fact a biennial, flowering the year after seed is sown, but it seeds itself freely and once established should never need to be replenished.

Mesembryanthemum criniflorum *Livingstone daisy.*

Mesembryanthemum criniflorum **Livingstone daisy**

Another South African daisy which has found popular use in the garden, the Livingstone daisy needs full sun and a dry soil to give of its best. Naturally a coastal plant, it can form great mats of low foliage several feet across, if left alone in a good site. This can be seen on the isle of Tresco in the Scilly Isles, as well as in its native home in the southern hemisphere. The low, spreading stems bear succulent leaves which have evolved to shed excessive salt on to their surfaces. The leaves, however, are almost covered by the 4 to 7cm (2 to 3in) flowers, in shades of pink, red, white and orange from July to September, if the plant is happy. Sow seed in trays in spring and plant out in May 20cm (8in) apart for a spectacular display on plants that never reach above 15cm (6in) in height.

Nicotiana alata *Tobacco flower.*

Nicotiana alata **Tobacco flower**

You have a choice with this plant – you may have colour through the day on compact plants just 25 to 45cm (10 to 18in) tall, or you may have wonderfully fragrant, white flowers which open only in the evening on plants that grow up to 1 to 1.3m (3 to 4ft) high. Or you can use both types, placing the latter towards the back of a border so that you do not have to put up with the rather straggly appearance of the plant below the loosely arranged flowers. Tobacco flowers thrive in any good garden soil, especially if it is well drained, in sun or light shade. They are best grown from seed, sown in trays in spring, to be planted out in May for flowering from June to October.

Nigella damascena **Love-in-a-mist**

This native of southern Europe appears at first glance to have leaves growing from the centre of the flowers. They are, in fact, thread-like bracts which originate from below the flower and come up around or through the petals. The flowers may be

Nigella damascena *Love-in-a-mist.*

single or double, in shades of blue, pink, maroon or white and are open from July to September, although earlier flowering can be achieved by sowing the seed in autumn, rather than spring. They may be sown in trays or where they are to flower and are fully hardy. They grow to 30 to 45cm (12 to 18in).

Papaver rhoeas *Field poppy.*

Papaver rhoeas Field poppy

One of only two native plants of northern and western Europe which produce red flowers, the field poppy can produce a spectacular display when seen en masse in a cornfield, but is equally worthwhile as a garden plant, where it can be appreciated individually and in close-up. It is one of numerous species and varieties which have been grown by gardeners over the centuries and is the parent of the famous Shirley poppies. Their dainty appearance belies their rugged nature and sowing seed where they are to flower in autumn will produce a crop of flowers which can be white, pink or the natural red, in single or double form from May to September on plants just 30 to 45cm (12 to 18in) tall. Deadheading is important to prolong flowering. They will thrive in any good garden soil, in sun or light shade.

Papaver somniferum *Opium poppy.*

Papaver somniferum Opium poppy

With its origins further east, in Greece and the Arab countries, the opium poppy reveals its tendency towards hotter climates by its grey stems and foliage, which grow up to 1m (3ft) tall or sometimes more. It is best grown in full sun, where it can show off its spectacular 8 to 10cm (3 to 4in) flowers to best advantage. Even then, however, the temperate climate of Britain is not sufficiently hot nor sunny to produce the drug for which the plant is named, and so the only non-decorative use it can be put to is in the thousands of seeds per seed head for use as decoration on home-made bread. However, the flowers – single or double and in colours from white through pinks, reds and mauves to deep purple – keep coming from June to September. The seed-heads are attractive, too, if left on, although this will shorten the flowering period.

Petunia hybrida Petunia

Like the lobelias, petunias come in bedding or trailing varieties, for use in borders or hanging baskets. They are half-hardy annuals and so should be sown in trays if your location is at any risk of frost. Sowing should be done in spring, for flowering from June to October. The broad trumpet flowers are held at the tips of soft, branching stems that, like the small leaves, are covered in fine hairs. The flowers may be up to 5cm (2in) or more across, single or double, in shades of white, pink, red or mauve. There is even a pale yellow variety now. They grow best in full sun, in any good garden soil. Dead-heading is important to prolong flowering and the plants can be cut back if they become straggly.

Petunia hybrida *Petunia*.

Rudbekia hirta *Rudbekia*.

Rudbekia hirta Rudbekia

Generally smaller than their perennial cousins, the annual rudbekias show the same raised, black or dark brown boss in the centre of the flower, surrounded by golden yellow sepals. (Technically, the daisies do not have petals, though this fine scientific point need not concern us as gardeners.) Similar to it, but with pink or mauve flowers, the closely related echinacea is another North American perennial which is well worth including in the seaside garden. The annual rudbekias can be sown as seed in April to flower from July to October, the plants reaching 30cm to 1m (1 to 3ft) in height. Dead-heading will prolong flowering. They prefer well-drained soil, in sun or light shade, and will grow well when tightly packed, like all natives of grassland.

Tagetes patula 'Tiger Eyes' French marigold

One of several species which have produced dozens of varieties between them of garden annuals. The group includes the larger African marigolds, the tiny-flowered tagetes and the French marigolds. All have finely-cut, mid- to dark-green foliage on sturdy plants topped by flowers which can now range from cream to dark red, but are mostly orange and were originally golden yellow. Flowers may be single or double and are produced prolifically over a long period from June to October, especially if dead-headed regularly. Plants grow to 15 to 27cm (6 to 9in) in any good garden soil. They prefer full sun. Seed can be sown in spring, in trays or where they are to flower.

Tagetes patula *'Tiger Eyes' French marigold.*

Tropaeolum majus *Nasturtium.*

Tropaeolum majus Nasturtium

There are compact varieties of this easy to grow plant for bedding and trailing ones for window boxes and hanging baskets. Varieties come in flower colours of cream, yellow, orange and red. The large seed can be sown where they are to flower in spring, or earlier in trays under glass, when the plants can be pinched out for bushiness when they are a finger-length tall. Flowering lasts from June to October, in sun or shade, and they tolerate any type of soil, but are best grown in poor ground, where they will put on less growth and more flower. Both the flowers and the rounded leaves are edible and can be used in salads.

Viola tricolor Heartsease

This small, dainty annual is a native of Britain and northern Europe. It is the parent plant of the numerous varieties of viola which are now available commercially everywhere, some with pure-coloured petals, some with whiskers and some with little faces, in any colour you can think of. They will grow in sun or light shade, producing small, compact plants up to 15cm (6in) in height, which can be cut back if they get straggly. They benefit from dead-heading to prolong flowering, which can be from April to October. Seed can be sown in spring, either under glass or where they are to flower, the plants growing well in any good garden soil.

Zinnia elegans *Zinnia.*

Zinnia elegans Zinnia

Like the tagetes and the dahlias which they can be taken to look like in flower, the zinnias come from Mexico and are not fully hardy, where frost is a problem. Therefore they are best sown under glass in early spring to produce sturdy plants that will flower from July to October. They like fertile but well-drained soil and require full sun to give of their best. The flowers, borne at the tops of plants from 15 to 60cm (6 to 24in) high, can be single, semi-double or fully double, in red, mauve, pink, cream or yellow, in single or bicolours and will put on a spectacular show if given the right conditions. Flowers can be anything from 5 to 15cm (2 to 6in) across.

Viola tricolor *Heartsease.*

There are many more annuals which make worthwhile additions to the seaside garden. Included among them are the following.

Ageratum		Low-growing, bushy plant with tufts of blue flowers summer and autumn. Needs to be kept watered.
Alyssum		Mat-forming rockery and wall plant, covered in yellow or white flower in spring and early summer.
Amaranthus caudatus	**Love-lies-bleeding**	Bushy annual with pale green, heart-shaped foliage and long, dark pink dangling panicles of tiny flowers in summer and autumn.
Bidens atrosanguinea		Now listed as *Cosmos atrosanguinea*, but still sold under the old name. Prostrate, branching plant, good for walls or hanging baskets. Feathery leaves and starry, yellow flowers through summer and autumn.
Borago officinalis	**Borage**	Hairy upright, branching plants with starry, bright blue flowers in summer.
Brachycome iberidifolia	**Swan-River daisy**	Prostrate, finely branched and narrow-leaved plant covered, in summer with yellow-centred, blue daisy flowers.
Calceolaria	**Slipper flower**	Compact, bushy plant with slightly hairy leaves and pouched flowers in reds, yellows and bicolours through late spring and summer.
Callistephus chinensis	**China aster**	Aster-like plants with flowers in red, pink, white or blue through summer and early autumn on plants up to 45cm (18in).
Campanula	**Bell flowers**	Huge group of annuals and perennials, from low, creeping types to tall, stately ones, all with blue or white flowers through the summer.
Cladanthus arabicus		A mound of light green, feathery foliage is dotted liberally with bright yellow daisy flowers in summer and early autumn. Up to 60cm (24in), like a yellow cosmos.
Consolida ambigua	**Larkspur**	Tall, stately plants with spires of blue, white or sometimes pink flowers through the summer. Very like the perennial delphiniums.
Dimorphotheca pluvialis	**Cape marigold**	Spreading plant with dark green leaves and wide, purple-backed, daisy flowers. Looks like the perennial osteospermum.
Felicia bergeriana	**Kingfisher daisy**	Mat of grey-green leaves densely covered in summer and early autumn with small, blue, daisy flowers that open in sunshine.
Helichrysum bracteatum	**Straw flower**	Upright, branching plant with mid-green, lanceolate leaves, topped by papery, daisy-like flowers in many colours, including red, pink, orange, white and yellow.
Helipterum manglesii		Similar to helichrysum, but greyish foliage and flowers in pink, red and white through summer and early autumn.
Ionopsidum acaule	**Violet cress**	One for a shadier spot. A low-growing edger or rockery plant with violet or white flowers in summer and early autumn.

Lathyrus odoratas	**Sweet pea**	Could equally be listed under climbers. Up to 2m (6ft) tall, grey-green stems and leaves with long-stemmed, fragrant flowers through the summer in many colours.
Linaria maroccana	**Toadflax**	Related to the perennial yellow and purple toadflaxes, these multi-coloured annuals grow to just 15cm (6in) tall, with small snapdragon-like flowers over a long season.
Lobularia maritime	**Sweet alyssum**	Spreading, grey-green mound-former with starry, white flowers in summer and early autumn.
Lupinus	**Lupins**	As well as the perennial forms, there are many annual varieties of this easy-to-grow plant, with flowers in many different colours. Pea-like flowers in tall plumes above deeply divided leaves.
Malcolmia maritime	**Virginia stock**	Upright, branching plants with dark, blue-green foliage topped with bright pink flowers through summer and early autumn.
Malope trifida	**Mallow**	Annual relative of the lavatera. Upright, branching bush of bright green foliage with many trumpet-shaped flowers in pink or white through summer and early autumn.
Nemesia strumosa	**Nemesia**	Fast grower, up to just 15cm (6in), with pale green lance-shaped leaves and deep-lipped flowers in various colours, including many bicolours, through the summer.
Nolana paradoxa		Low-growing, prostrate plant for the rockery or edging. Light green leaves and blue trumpet flowers with yellow throats in summer.
Perilla frutescens		Mainly grown for the aromatic red-purple leaves, it also bears spikes of tiny white flowers in summer. Up to 60cm (2ft).
Platystemon californicus	**Cream cups**	Pale yellow, buttercup flowers cover this bushy greyish-green plant through the summer.
Reseda odorata	**Mignonette**	Bushy light green plant with oval leaves and conical heads of tiny, fragrant, white flowers in summer and early autumn.
Salpiglosis sinuata		Widely flared, trumpet flowers in many colours, often with contrasting veining on bushy plants up to 60cm (2ft) tall through the summer.
Schitzopetalon walkeri		Upright, mid-green plant to 45cm (18in) with deeply divided leaves and almond-scented, white flowers with deeply cut and fringed petals through the summer.
Schizanthus	**Butterfly flower**	Large, brightly coloured, orchid-like flowers in profusion through summer and into autumn on plants up to 45cm (18in) tall.
Tolpis barbata		Branching plant up to 60cm (2ft) tall with serrated, lanceolate leaves and bright yellow, daisy flowers with purple centres in summer.
Ursinia anthemoides		Bushy, feathery-leaved, pale green annual with large, bright yellow gazania-like, daisy flowers with a maroon ring at the base of the outer petals. Height 30cm (12in), flowering through summer and autumn.

CHAPTER 5

Perennials

Perennials may loosely be described as those plants that live for more than a single year. This includes biennials, which are sometimes separated out because, in the natural situation, they live for just two years, dying after setting seed. Foxgloves, wall-flowers, daisies and echiums are common examples of this type. They have been included here because they can be used in the garden as short-lived perennials. By diligently dead-heading them before they can seed, one can make them live for another year, and another and sometimes even another.

Bulbs (including corms, which often look similar to bulbs and have the same function, but are of different physiological origin) are often used in the garden in the same way as annuals, in that they are planted out, flower and are then removed from the border. However, bulbs and corms do not die when they have flowered. They recede into their storage organ and survive for another year. Gardeners often have them do this in a dried-off state in the shed, rather than their taking up space in the borders, but in many cases this is not necessary for the benefit of the plants themselves. They tend to be useful in the seaside garden because they have narrow, strap-like leaves and so are not affected too much by wind. Furthermore, those leaves last for just a few weeks every year and then are shed, so that the plants are less affected by the salty atmosphere on the coast than some others might be.

Perennials are generally considered to be plants that survive for several years but die back to ground level each winter, having soft, sappy stems rather than woody ones. They can be as brightly colourful as the annuals, but take longer to reach flowering size from seed. They can achieve a larger size than many of the annuals because they have the advantage of already having an established rootstock at the start of the growing season, after their first year.

This is best demonstrated by those plants which have perennial and annual forms, such as the yarrows. Annual types tend to be small, perhaps only a few centimetres high, while their perennial cousins may reach to over a metre and a quite substantial bulk.

The fact that they die back in winter (although some leave dead stems and seed heads behind, which can be attractive in those areas where frost is prevalent) is an advantage in exposed sites such as those found on the coast. And perennial plants are less work for the gardener, especially in spring; they may need to be dug up and divided every few years, as they get dense and congested or simply too large for their position, but this can be done in the autumn or spring and it also has the advantage of providing more plants in the process. The patient gardener can therefore fill his plot over the course of three or four years for very little money. A new garden can thus be started with a lot of annuals for instant effect, with a few perennials mixed in, which will bulk up over the coming years, be split and planted back to fill the borders gradually and reduce the workload.

As with the annuals, diligent dead-heading can

Sea kale, Crambe maritima, smothers itself in small, fragrant white flowers and thrives in the poorest of soils.

prolong the flowering season of perennial plants quite extensively, and some, such as the hardy geraniums, will flower twice in a year if clipped back hard after the first crop. Including those perennials which are often sold and used as annuals, such as the pansies, antirrhinums and primroses, as well as the bulbs, you can have perennial plants in flower virtually every month of the year – especially in a coastal garden, where the weather is generally milder than inland.

suitable to grow next to it (the achilleas – yarrows – make a good choice), it certainly makes a bold statement in the garden. It dislikes disturbance but may be lifted and divided in the autumn, when clumps get too large. Easily available from garden centres, it can also be grown from seed, sown under glass in spring or autumn.

Agapanthus africanus *African lily.*

Acanthus spinosus *Bear's britches.*

Acanthus spinosus **Bear's britches**
A native of southern Europe, this 1.2m (4ft) plant has spiny, deeply cut, dark green leaves which are highly ornamental on their own. It bears tall spikes of purple and white flowers from June to October, thriving in sun or light shade, although it prefers a well-drained site. The firm stems need no staking and, although it may be difficult to find something

Agapanthus africanus **African lily**
These exotic-looking, South African bulbs are hardier than one might think from their appearance, especially in a seaside garden. The rosettes of strap-shaped, mid-green, glossy leaves throw erect flower spikes up to 1m (3ft) tall, between July and September, at the top of which buds open to produce firework balls of 5cm (2in), rich blue or white trumpet flowers. Unlike the camassia, which looks

broadly similar, although the flowers are in short spikes, rather than balls, the African lily does need some protection if frost is a problem in your garden, but it is well worth growing in a sunny, well-drained site. It flowers even better if crammed into a restricted space. Bulbs are available from garden centres.

and even multicoloured leaves. It flowers from May to August, grows in any good garden soil, in sun or shade and is readily available from all the usual sources. It can be propagated from seed, sown either under glass or where it is to grow, or by division in spring or autumn.

Ajuga reptans *Bugle*.

Alchemilla mollis *Lady's mantle*.

Ajuga reptans **Bugle**

Low and unobtrusive, this native of Britain and northern Europe is a tough, ground-cover plant which has become popular in the garden, especially since several garden hybrids have been introduced. The basic plant is mid- to dark green, with gentian-blue flowers in short spikes, up to 15cm (6in) high, but there are now purple-leaved and white-flowered forms as well as several with variegated

Alchemilla mollis **Lady's mantle**

A classic of the cottage garden, lady's mantle is equally at home in a modern dry garden. The clump of wide, light green leaves are hairy and soft and look wonderful after rain, when they hold glistening drops on their surfaces, like balls of mercury in the sun. The flowers are borne in fine sprays of light yellow, up to 45cm (18in) tall from June to August. Preferring a well-drained soil, it can tolerate sun or shade and is easily grown from seed, sown in autumn or spring as well as being readily available from garden centres and nurseries. Clumps may be lifted and divided in late spring.

Allium schoenoprasum *Chives.*

Allium schoenoprasum Chives
This long-flowering, hardy herb with its 30cm (1ft)-long, narrow, onion-flavoured leaves and little balls of dark pink flowers up to 2.5cm (1in) across, has long been a staple of British and European gardens. There is a white-flowered form and a larger variety, up to one and a half times the size. Along with most others of the onion family, chives grow well in a well-drained soil, in a sunny site, although they can tolerate some light shade. Dying right back in winter if left outdoors, chives may be dug up and brought indoors to provide winter flavour for culinary use. Otherwise, they come up afresh in spring and are ready for picking by April. Dead-heading will prolong flowering, which lasts from May to July. Readily available from all the usual sources, the clumps thicken quickly and can be lifted and divided in autumn. Seed can be sown in spring or autumn.

Anemone × hybrida *Japanese anemone.*

Anemone × hybrida Japanese anemone
Several named varieties of this herbaceous perennial are available, with flower colours ranging from white through pink to red and some double examples too. The plants grow to 0.7 to 1.4m (2 to 4ft) in any good garden soil, in sun or semi-shade. Once established, they will spread to form large clumps, which can be lifted and divided in spring, or root cuttings taken in winter. The number of varieties is an indication of its popularity and therefore the ease of acquiring this plant commercially. It can also be grown from seed, sown in spring under glass for flowering the following year.

Anthemis tinctora *Marguerite.*

Anthemis tinctora **Marguerite**

Hardier than it looks, the plant is a British native, although it has been bred for garden use into a number of varieties, with flowers ranging from white to rich yellow and leaves from grey to deep green. The foliage is light and feathery, the flowers borne above it, 2.5cm (1in)-wide daisies. Its open, branching habit endears it to many gardeners. It flowers from June to September, growing to 0.7 to 1m (2 to 3ft) tall. Plants are available from garden centres and nurseries. Seed can be sown in autumn or spring.

Aquilegia vulgaris *Columbine.*

Aquilegia vulgaris **Columbine**

Like the alliums, the aquilegias range right across the northern hemisphere. They prefer a well-drained soil, but can tolerate sun or shade. They flower from April to early July, the flowers borne high on stalks up to 1m (3ft) tall, above light green, lobed foliage which rises in clumps from the ground. Self-seeding readily in the garden, they are easily raised from seed and planted where you wish. Plants are also available from the usual sources. The flowers can come in various sizes, from 3cm (1¼in) to 6cm (2½in) and in assorted colours, from white through pink to darkest purple and yellow as well as red and even a light blue. Tougher than they look, they can tolerate just about any weather conditions without the need for staking.

Armeria maritima *Thrift.*

Armeria maritima **Thrift**

The classic seaside plant, this native of Britain and western Europe is grown in gardens from the coast to the Midlands in Britain. Also available in white-flowered and variegated forms, the native bears pink blobs of flower about 1cm (½in) across, on short stalks above the pincushion of soft, grassy foliage from May to July. It looks much like a miniature version of chives from a distance, but is spreading, rather than clump-forming, and without any scent. Available from garden centres and nurseries everywhere, it can be propagated from seed in spring or autumn, or by rooting small cuttings in autumn.

Astrantia major *Masterwort.*

Astrantia major Masterwort

A flower for those shady spots in any garden, masterwort is happiest in a moisture-retentive soil, although it looks as if it should be grown in a sunny, dry garden. The stiff, pincushion flowers, in shades from metallic green to deep red, can be up to 3cm (1½in) across, on stiff, narrow stems above deeply divided foliage which is naturally mid-green although there are a number of variegated varieties available. Commonly used as a dried flower, it blooms in high summer at a height of 30 to 60cm (1 to 2ft). Available from garden centres and nurseries, it can also be grown from seed sown in spring. Clumps can be lifted and divided in spring or autumn.

Aubretia deltoidea Aubretia

Native to the northern Mediterranean, this wall and rockery classic has graced the gardens of Britain for hundreds of years and is widely grown elsewhere for its tough constitution, low, spreading habit, tidy manner and long flowering period, from

Aubretia deltoidea *Aubretia.*

March to June. A plant of grey-green foliage and small purple flowers, there are also varieties with white, mauve or near-red flowers, one with double flowers, some with silver or gold variegation on the leaves. It will spread up to 60cm (2ft), but attains only about 10cm (4in) in height, the flowers being roughly 1.5cm (½in) across and smothering the plant while it is in bloom. Readily available from all the usual sources, it is also easily grown from seed, sown in spring or summer, or from cuttings in autumn. Division can also be carried out at this time of year.

Bellis perennis *Daisy.*

Bellis perennis **Daisy**

One of the longest-flowering herbaceous plants of all, the little, white-petalled blooms with their rich yellow centres can be seen in lawns and road verges in almost any month of the year, although they are most floriferous in spring and early summer. These pretty, if sometimes unwelcome, natives have been bred for garden use into 2.5cm (1in)-wide pom-poms of double flower in red, pink or white, which can be used for bedding or edging and will not self-seed, as they are a sterile form. Happy in sun or light shade, they prefer a soil that retains some moisture. They can be lifted and divided in autumn and can be bought from all the usual sources, especially in spring.

Canna × generalis *Canna.*

Canna × *generalis* **Canna**

Native to central America, these exotic-looking, rhizomatous plants are usually considered non-hardy, although trials are being carried out now to see whether they will survive a British winter in the ground. This is more likely in a relatively frost-free site and with a bed of sharp grit under the rhizome and more mixed into the earth around it. Dahlias, coming from similar locations, may certainly be left in the ground and survive all but the harshest winters, thus there is hope for the cannas. If in doubt, cut plants down at the first sign of frost and dry off indoors for the winter, planting up again under glass in early spring. They grow to anything up to 1.2m (4ft), with broad, lush foliage that may be mid-green or bronze, sometimes with variegations and large flowers in reds, yellows and oranges, with petals up to 10cm (4in) long. Flowers are borne in short panicles at the top of a thick stem from mid-summer to early autumn. Rhizomes can be divided in spring, when the shoots show, each section needing at least one shoot. Plants are available from garden centres either as rhizomes or in growth.

Carlina *Ornamental thistle.*

Carlina **Ornamental thistle**

Although the group contains some voracious weeds of field and garden, the thistles also number among themselves some highly ornamental, herbaceous perennials. Closely related to the popular garden plant *Morina longifolia*, some of them are equally attractively variegated of leaf, with pink or mauve flowers held high in the sun. Thriving in a well-drained site, they prefer a sunny location. Dead-heading (preferably with gloves) can prolong flowering and prevent self-seeding – which never come true in any case. Flowering is from early summer to autumn. Plants are available from nurseries and some larger garden centres.

Crambe maritima *Sea kale.*

Crambe maritima Sea kale

Grown mainly for its rounded, wavy-edged leaves, whose spring shoots can be eaten as a vegetable, sea kale can have light green or greyish foliage, which is lost in summer beneath finely branching sprays of tiny white flowers, much like gypsophilla, which is another plant worthy of a seaside garden. Naturally a coastal plant, as its name suggests, it enjoys a sunny, well-drained site and provides a worthy addition to the garden, whether in flower or not. Available from nurseries and some coastal garden centres, it can also be grown from seed sown in spring or from root cuttings in the same season.

Cyclamen hederifolium *Cyclamen.*

Cyclamen hederifolium Cyclamen

Originating around the Mediterranean, the cyclamens are mostly hardy. *C. hederifolium* is among these, with its heart-shaped leaves, variegated with silver above and deep red beneath, carried from winter to late spring. It flowers from August to November, preferring a shady or semi-shaded site and well-drained soil. The older the tuber, the more flowers it will tend to produce. In common with that other classic of dappled shade, the snow-drop, cyclamen prefers to be moved in the green – with leaves on, rather than as dried corms. Commonly available from all the usual sources, they can be grown from seed, although there is no guarantee of flower colour with this method. Flowers can be white, pink or mauve and are up to 1.5cm (¾in) long, borne on stalks up to 10cm (4in) tall.

Dahlia *Dahlia.*

Dahlia Dahlia

These semi-hardy perennials from Mexico should be safe to leave in the ground through the winter in coastal gardens, although many gardeners inland lift them and store them as dried tubers indoors through the winter, once the frost has killed off the foliage and semi-succulent stems. The leaves are toothed ovals of mid- to dark green, except for the few varieties that have bronze leaves. Flowers are so various it is impracticable to list all the choices, in reds, yellows, pinks and oranges, double, cactus-flowered, pom-pom and semi-double, on plants which can range from 30cm (1ft) to 1.5m (5ft) tall. Grow them in a sunny or semi-shaded spot, in a rich, well-fertilized soil. Pinching out the tips when the plants are young improves branching and therefore flower production. Taller types need some form of staking for the support of the large, heavy flowers. Readily available from all the usual sources.

Dianthus deltoides *Maiden pink.*

Dianthus deltoides Maiden pink

The maiden pink is one of the alpine pinks, as opposed to the border varieties, which are larger, with more double flowers. Also related to the sweet william and the annual carnations, the maiden pink is one of a group of flowers that have been in cultivation for thousands of years. They were known and loved by the ancient Greeks. Darker than many of its relatives, the maiden pink has the same grassy foliage, but a mat-forming habit, rather than the clumping habit of many of its cousins. All are happy in a sunny position and a well-drained soil, although the maiden pink can tolerate semi-shade. The flowers are 1cm (½in) across, held up to 15cm (6in) high and a deep vermilion above dark green foliage. It can easily be found in garden centres and nurseries, can be sown from seed in spring or autumn or be lifted and divided in autumn.

Cuttings of all the pinks are easily rooted. A non-flowering spur is simply placed in a well-drained compost or even in a jar of water in a shady spot and roots will appear in a few weeks.

Diascia cordata *Diascia.*

Diascia cordata Diascia

Another of those perennials that is often listed among the annuals because that is the way it is used in gardens outside its native South Africa, the diascia is surprisingly hardy and can remain outdoors over winter, even in an inland garden in Britain. However, it is happiest in a milder, coastal climate, with a sunny spot and a well-drained soil, where it can lift its white, pink, red or mauve flowers, up to 1cm (½in) across in spikes up to 20cm (8in) tall over felty, grey-green leaves. A bushier plant will be produced if you pinch out the growing tip when the young plant is just 5cm (2in) high and flowering will be extended if you dead-head regularly. Readily found in garden centres and nurseries, it may also be grown from seed, sown under glass in February.

Dietes grandiflora *Cape iris.*

Dietes grandiflora Cape iris

This South African relative of the iris (many of which also make excellent subjects for the coastal garden) is a clump-forming evergreen with sword-shaped, dark green leaves, up to 1m (3ft) long, above which it bears its white flowers, up to 10cm (4in) across, for several weeks in summer. A rhizomatous plant, it can take full sun or light shade and prefers a dryish position. Water regularly but sparingly. It is not fully frost-hardy but should do well in most coastal gardens and provide a spectacular show, especially if planted close to a path, where its flowers may be enjoyed close to. Available only from some specialist nurseries outside South Africa, it can be grown from seed or propagated by division of its rhizome in spring. Lift the plant and use a sharp knife to cut off sections of rhizome, each with a spray of leaves and a little root. Cut the leaves down to about 15cm (6in) long and replant at or close to the surface, as you would the iris.

Echeveria elegans

These rosette-forming, perennial succulents need a well-drained site in full sun to give their best. Not hardy, they will tolerate cold if kept on the dry side, but may be killed by hard frosts. However, they will tolerate the salt-laden, drying air of the coast well and the flower spikes, in reds and oranges, last for many weeks in summer and early autumn. An ideal subject for pots or the rockery or for growing on walls. Usually sold as a house plant, it is available from many garden centres and nurseries and can be easily propagated from seed or from leaf cuttings in

Echeveria elegans.

spring. It also puts out offsets which can be allowed to root, then cut away for planting elsewhere.

Epilobium angustifolium alba White rosebay willowherb

The rosebay willowherb is a native of Britain and northern Europe, where it spreads readily, especially in disturbed ground, to form masses of 1m (3ft)-tall, fine-leaved, upright stems, topped through the late summer with delicate pink flowers. A little too vigorous for most gardens, its white-flowered form is much more manageable in habit, tending to form well-defined clumps. The main job associated with this plant, once it is established, is the annual task of removing self-set seedlings from around it. Happy in most soils, in sun or semi-shade, it is increasingly available from garden centres and nurseries. Clumps can be lifted and divided in spring or autumn, but collected seed will often revert to the native pink type.

Epilobium angustifolium alba *White rosebay willowherb.*

Erigeron speciosus *Fleabane.*

Erigeron speciosus Fleabane

Growing naturally all across the northern hemisphere, the erigerons have a plant to suit most situations, be it in sun or shade, tall or low-growing, but they tend to like a well-drained position. The open, daisy flowers tend to come in shades of pink, mauve or purple, with prominent yellow central bosses. There are numerous varieties and several species grown in the garden, some for the border and others for the rockery. Fully hardy, they will self-seed freely where they are happy and are commonly grown in seaside gardens for their toughness and ability to flower profusely over a long period in summer; the taller varieties are often mistaken for the aster or Michaelmas daisy. Available from all the usual sources, they can be easily grown from seed. Clumps can be divided in spring.

Eryngium × oliverianum *Sea holly.*

Eryngium × *oliverianum* **Sea holly**

Another wide-ranging group of species from Europe, Asia and South and Central America, the eryngiums are not all coastal in nature and not all hardy. They were named for their British native member, *Eryngium maritima*, which is a worthy garden plant with a height of 45cm (18in) that grows naturally on our coasts. *E. oliverianum* is a taller garden variety, reaching 1m (3ft). Its flowers are more mauve than the metallic blue of the native species, but still with the distinctive, thistle-like heads surrounded by deeply divided bracts of the same colour. The leaves are rounded and blue-green. Flowering is from July to September. Plants are readily available commercially and the species can be sown from seed, although the varieties will not come true. They dislike root disturbance and thus lifting and division are done solely to reinvigorate dense clumps.

Eucomis autumnalis *Pineapple lily.*

Eucomis autumnalis **Pineapple lily**

Not fully hardy inland, the pineapple lily is often grown in coastal gardens, where its distinctive structure always creates interest. Originating in South Africa like so many of our garden plants, it is a bulbous perennial which produces a rosette of strap-shaped leaves, from the centre of which rises a flower spike up to 45cm (18in) in height. The 2cm (¾in) blooms open widely all around the stem in a hyacinth-like column, which is topped by the tuft of leafy bracts that give the plant its common name. There are several species and varieties in the group, but *E. autumnalis* is among the hardier and easier

ones to find. Available from some garden centres and nurseries, you may have to search, although it is more commonly sold near the coast. It prefers a light soil in a sunny spot. Plant the bulbs 15 to 20cm (6 to 8in) deep and use a thick mulch over winter if your site suffers from cold weather.

Euphorbia amygdaloides *Wood spurge.*

Euphorbia amygdaloides **Wood spurge**

The euphorbias are one of the largest groups of plants, along with the daisies, and are found naturally all over the world. Some are hardy, some not, but almost all are interesting in some way, if your conditions suit them. Like all the herbaceous examples (there are also shrubby and succulent ones), the wood spurge exudes an irritant, milky sap when cut. Happy in dry soil, in a semi-shaded or shady spot, the wood spurge is a European and

British native which has been taken into garden use. There are now several varieties, but they all grow to around 45 to 60cm (18 to 24in), the stems all rising from the basal crown and surrounded by narrow leaves. At the tops come flower heads in red, orange or yellow which last for a long time on the plant from their opening in spring. There are red-stemmed and purple-leaved varieties, among others, and, as evergreens, they are a useful addition to the border.

Galanthus nivalis *Snowdrop.*

Galanthus nivalis Snowdrop
Snowdrops are among the earliest harbingers of the new season in the garden. Originating across Europe, there are several species, but all look quite similar from a distance. With over a hundred species and varieties now in cultivation, there are gardens which are famous for these hardy little bulbous plants alone. Give them some shelter and a rich, loamy soil and, once established, they will do you well. However, it is a waste of time and money to buy them as dry bulbs. They are best planted when in the green – just after the flowers have faded but with the leaves still intact. Available from all the usual sources, they can also be sown from seed, although the varieties will not come true in this way. Seed should be sown fresh, in damp compost. Clumps can be lifted and divided after flowering, in March or April.

Galtonia candicans Summer hyacinth
These African bulbs can reach anything from 60 to 120cm (2 to 4ft), with the single, erect flower stem carrying a multitude of white blooms from July to

Galtonia candicans *Summer hyacinth.*

September, and provide a good filler for the middle or the back of the border or between shrubs. The best impact is achieved by planting in clumps of three or more. Plant at least 15cm (6in) deep in spring. Though they thrive best in full sun, they can tolerate semi-shade in any reasonable garden soil; however, they dislike disturbance. Bulbs are available from garden centres and nurseries.

Helianthemum nummularium Rock rose
Native to Britain and Europe, these are, in fact, tiny shrubs. They are evergreen with pale to mid-green leaves and flowers in a wide variety of colours, borne profusely from May to July. Liking a sunny position, they can tolerate any good garden soil, although they prefer it well drained. With a height of just 15cm (6in), they can spread by up to four times that length, with flowers up to 2.5cm (1in) across. They are readily available in garden centres and nurseries and can be propagated from cuttings in summer.

Helianthemum nummularium *Rock rose.*

Hemerocallis *Day lily.*

Hemerocallis **Day lily**

Named for the fact that its lily-like flowers, though borne profusely over a long period, last for only a day. They originate in China and Japan and there are numerous crosses with several flower colours from creamy white to dark red through yellows and oranges, some with bicoloured petals. The tufts of sword-shaped leaves throw flower stems up to 75cm (2½ft) tall from June to August. They are equally at home in sun or shade and in dry or damp soil. Plant between October and April, which is also when clumps may be lifted and divided, if necessary. They are readily available from nurseries and garden centres.

Heuchera *Coral flower.*

Heuchera **Coral flower**

There are several named varieties of the coral flower, an American native plant with leaves varying from greyish green through dark green and marbled to dark purple. The rosettes of low-growing, rounded, evergreen leaves reach only a few centimetres in height, but from June to August they throw up slender stems of tiny red, pink or orange, bell-shaped flowers in fine sprays to 60cm (2ft) tall. Growing in sun or light shade, they can thrive in any good garden soil. They are readily available from garden centres and nurseries and can be lifted and divided in spring or autumn.

Knautia macedonica *Greek scabious.*

Liatris spicata *Gay Feather.*

Liatris callilepsis Gay Feather

This reliable American clump-forming plant has small, dark pink flowers in dense spikes up to 30cm (12in) long, above tufts of spiky foliage through late summer and early autumn. Flowering well on poor soil, it prefers a sunny, well-drained location. It is closely related to the commonly available *L. Spicata*, which is used in bog gardens and moist soil. The species will grow to 1m (3ft) in height, though there is a smaller variety call 'Kobold' that attains just 65cm (2ft) in height. Easily available in garden centres as growing plants or in tuber form, they can also be grown from seed, though this is not often seen for sale. Seed harvested in the garden can be sown in autumn or spring. Plants can be lifted and divided in spring, every three years or so.

Knautia macedonica Greek scabious

The greyish, felty leaves with their sharply divided edges are evergreen and the 2.5cm (1in) pink or dark red flowers are borne in profusion on thin, divided stems from June to October. Deadheading extends flowering and prevents the tendency to self-seed copiously. It is best planted among other tall plants that can lend the rather lax flower stems some support. The Greek scabious and many of its close relatives can be found in garden centres and nurseries everywhere. They can be lifted and divided in autumn or self-set seedlings transplanted in autumn or spring. They prefer a sunny spot in any good garden soil, on a dryish site.

Kniphofia uvularia *Red-hot poker.*

Limonium latifolium *Sea lavender.*

Kniphofia uvularia **Red-hot poker**

Clumps of stiff, grass-like, evergreen foliage mark this South African plant in the border. There are numerous varieties with different flower colours, from cream to red and not all display the classic colour fade from one tone to another up the spike. Also variable are the flowering time and the height, so some care is required when choosing this plant in the garden centre or nursery. They are generally from 45cm to 1.5m (18in to 4½ft) in height, flowering from July to September, although some are earlier. Commonly available, they can be lifted and divided in spring and prefer a sunny, well-drained position.

Limonium latifolium **Sea lavender**

The semi-evergreen foliage is broad and glossy, somewhat like 25cm (9in) green tongues growing in a low, unremarkable mound. Then, in summer, the flower stems begin to rise. Like pink gypsophilla, the finely cut and much-branched thin stems form a ball of netting up to 75cm (2½ft) tall which is covered with tiny flowers. These pale pink or lavender blossoms can be cut and dried for indoor use. The plant is fully hardy and grows naturally in poor, dry soils in full sun and in the drying, salty winds of the coast. It is available from nurseries and some garden centres and can be sown from seed, but is not suited to lifting and division.

Linum perene *Flax.*

Linum perene **Flax**

Like the sea lavender, flax is a native of Britain and western Europe. Flax is noted, however, for its wiry stems with tiny, narrow leaves in mid-green, topped in summer with sky-blue flowers up to 1cm (0.4in) across, which it bears profusely. The plants are up to 45cm (18in) tall and herbaceous, dying down to ground level in winter. It prefers a sunny site with a dry soil. Not the longest-living plant in the garden, it is readily available from nurseries and some garden centres and is easily propagated from seed or summer cuttings.

Macleaya cordata *Plume poppy.*

Macleaya cordata **Plume poppy**

This is one native of China and Japan which makes a bold statement. Not one for the small border, it tends to spread by suckering underground; but if you have the space for it, the large, deeply divided leaves, greyish or bronze above and felted beneath, are attractive for most of the year. In summer they are topped by plumes up to 1m (3ft) long of white, pinkish or buff-coloured, loosely arranged tiny flowers that reach to well over head height. Preferring a moist soil, it likes a sunny position but can tolerate partial shade. Clumps can be divided in autumn or spring, or root cuttings taken in spring. The plants are available from nurseries.

Miscanthus sinensis *Chinese silver grass.*

Miscanthus sinensis **Chinese silver grass**

Several forms of this decorative native of China and Japan have been bred since its introduction to Europe in the mid-nineteenth century, some with silver streaks and others with purple in the leaves. They grow to between 60 and 120cm (2 to 4ft) and are topped in summer with waving plumes of whitish flower heads. Not quite an evergreen but still decorative in winter if the old stems are left on until the new shoots begin to appear from the base in early spring. They are tolerant plants which can thrive in sun or light shade, in damp or dry soil. They quickly form a sizeable clump which can be lifted and divided in spring or autumn and are readily available from nurseries.

Muscari racemosum *Grape hyacinth.*

Muscari racemosum **Grape hyacinth**

The narrow, mid-green, grass-like leaves of this native of Britain and western Europe are topped by bright blue spikes of tiny flowers up to 3cm (1¼in)

long in March and April, when they can form a pleasing contrast with daffodils and tulips, sitting under either to provide a mass of colour for several weeks. They quickly increase by offsets once established and can be dug up and divided as dry bulbs in autumn. Preferring a sunny site in well-drained soil, they can reach 30cm (1ft) in height. Bulbs are available from all the usual sources.

Nerine bowdenii *Nerine.*

Nerine bowdenii **Nerine**

Another South African which has found a home in gardens everywhere, this is just one of several species of nerine, but the hardiest. It likes a warm, sunny location in well-drained soil where its bulbs, sitting on the soil surface, can bake in the sun. Flower spikes come up in autumn, to be topped late in the year with rings of delicate pink flowers, whose long, narrow petals and stamens combine to look like over-sized honeysuckle flowers, each up to 5cm (2in) across. The leaves come after the flowers have faded and are narrow and strap-shaped, providing a splash of mid-green through the winter. Available from nurseries and garden centres, they can be lifted and divided in spring if the clumps get too congested.

Oenothera odorata sulphurea *Evening primrose.*

Oenothera odorata sulphurea **Evening primrose**

A member of another wide-ranging genus of plants from Britain and Europe through Asia, and North and South America, *O. odorata sulphurea* comes from South America. Its red-tinted leaves are topped with lemon-yellow flowers up to 5cm (2in) across, on plants up to 60cm (2ft) tall. The flowers open in the evening from June to September. The plants prefer a sunny site on well-drained ground. They are readily found in garden centres and nurseries and easily raised from seed sown in spring.

Osteospermum ecklonis *Cape daisy.*

Osteospermum ecklonis **Cape daisy**

There are several members of the *Osteospermum* family grown in gardens, but *O. ecklonis* is probably the hardiest and certainly one of the prettiest with its blue-backed, white petals around a dark centre with tiny gold spots circling its rim. The foliage is dark green, the leaves having crinkled edges and the plant forms substantial clumps in time if grown in a sunny, well-drained spot. A native of South Africa, it is well suited to a coastal situation. Up to 60cm (2ft) tall in flower and blooming from late June to September, it is well worth inclusion in any garden. It is readily available from all the usual places and can be propagated from cuttings of non-flowering shoots in summer.

Papaver orientalis **Oriental poppy**

The deep-cut, hairy, grey-green leaves of this native of the Black Sea region make it look as if it ought to be growing in a coastal location and, indeed, it does suit a dry, sunny location and is well able to withstand the salty, drying winds of a seaside garden. Coming fresh each spring, the luxuriant clumps of foliage are topped by stiff, hairy stems in May and June, which bear the large, open flowers singly. Up to 15cm (6in) across, the flowers come in a wide range of colours from white through yellow and orange to deepest red and even purple and last much longer than they look as if they should, with their delicate, paper petals. Commonly available commercially, it can be propagated from root cuttings in winter or spring. Although dead-heading is advisable after flowering and can lead to a small second

Papaver orientalis *Oriental poppy.*

Phygelius capensis *Cape fuchsia.*

flowering in September if the weather is mild, it can also be sown from seed in spring. Varieties will not come true in this way, however.

Phygelius capensis **Cape fuchsia**

Tall, slender spires of flame-red or pink 3.5cm (1½in) flowers rise above the triangular, dark green leaves of this substantial plant through summer and early autumn. Technically a shrub, it generally dies back to ground level in winter, as do many of the fuchsias from which it gets one of its common names. Cut back almost to ground level in early spring, it will grow again to 1 to 1.3m (3 to 4ft) before flowering. It prefers an open, sunny site in well-drained but not too dry soil. Fully hardy, it is available from many garden centres and nurseries and can be easily propagated from summer cuttings of shoot tips.

Polemonium caeruleum *Jacob's ladder.*

Polemonium caeruleum Jacob's ladder
This native of Britain and Europe also has relatives in the USA and Mexico. Named for the ladder-like formation of its leaflets, set at right angles up the central rib, there are variegated and white-flowered varieties as well as pink-flowered ones, but the original plant has blue flowers with golden yellow anthers, grows to 45cm (18in) tall and flowers through the summer, the flowering being prolonged by dead-heading. Once flowering is over, the stems can be cut back to ground level and a tuft of new leaves will appear to reinvigorate the plant for a possible second flush of flowers in early autumn. It prefers a well-drained site, but can tolerate some moisture at its feet and will grow in sun or light shade. A good filler between other plants, it will benefit from their support if the site is not sheltered. It is available from many garden centres and nurseries. Established clumps can be lifted and divided in spring or autumn, or seed sown in late summer.

Potentilla atrosanguineum *Cinquefoil.*

Potentilla atrosanguineum Cinquefoil
Closely related to the shrubby potentillas used as hedging plants, these evergreen, herbaceous plants form low-growing tufts of strawberry-like foliage, from which rise slender, branching flower stems throughout the summer. The 2.5cm (1in), wide open, round flowers come in a range of colours from yellow, through orange to dark burgundy and include some bicolours. The flower stems are rather

lax, but can give a bright splash to the border when grown in a clump. The plant enjoys a well-drained, sunny site. Clumps can be divided in spring or autumn and new plants are available from all the usual sources.

Primula *Primrose.*

Primula Primrose
There are many members of the *Primula* family, thriving in all kinds of situation, from dry to wet and sun to shade and giving just about any flower colour you might wish for; but here we are discussing those multi-coloured hybrids of the common primrose. Looking sometimes like a larger-flowered variety of that native British plant of shady hedgerows and woodland edges, which is itself a worthy addition to any garden, they come in a wide variety of shades, both single and multi-coloured, some with double flowers. All prefer a degree of shade for at least part of the day, although any reasonable garden soil will do. Available everywhere you could think of buying plants from, they will not come true from seed, but mixed packets are available. The trick with these is to give them a cold snap before sowing – a couple of weeks in the refrigerator works wonders – and sow them outdoors, the fresher the better.

Salvia *Sage.*

Sedum acer *Stonecrop.*

Sedum acer Stonecrop

There are both rockery and border plants within this fleshy-leaved group, of which two are mentioned here. The stonecrops are rockery flowers, with blooms in yellow, red or white, according to variety. This one is a native of Britain and Europe and one of the best carpet formers of all. It grows to just a few centimetres tall, but spreads more than 60cm (2ft), if allowed to, and is covered with starry flowers through the height of summer. Needing a dry root-run and preferring full sun, it is a good plant for a dry patch where height is not needed. Available from garden centres and nurseries, it can also be propagated from seed in spring or autumn and from cuttings.

Salvia Sage

Another almost world-wide family of plants, there is a sage from almost any country to suit almost any garden situation. Some are culinary herbs, some shrubs grown for their leaf colour and others either annuals or perennials grown for their flowers, in red, purple or blue, though there are now some pink- and even white-flowered varieties. Generally speaking, the sages enjoy a fairly dry root-run and plenty of sun and have been used in the gardens of the world for so long that they can provide an excellent choice of plant for any spot you have to spare in a coastal garden. Many are easy from cuttings and most are available from the usual sources.

Sedum spectabile *Iceplant.*

Sedum spectabile Iceplant

This much taller sedum is used in the herbaceous border and is widely known for its ability to attract bees. Growing to 45 to 60cm (1½ to 2ft), the succulent, light green or greyish stems and leaves are topped by broad panicles of tiny pink or red flowers in high summer. There is also a variety with pink foliage and dark red flowers. The plants die back to ground level in winter, maintaining just a low tuft of leaves, but the flower stems stay on, though dead, to provide some height and interest until they are cut off in spring to allow room for the new year's growth. Available as plants from all the usual sources, they can be sown as seed in spring or autumn.

Silene maritima Sea campion

Another classic seaside plant of both wild places and gardens, the sea campion is often regarded as a subspecies of the taller bladder campion, which is found inland, but also enjoys a sunny site and well-drained soil. The sea campion, however, grows to just 15cm (6in) in height and has fleshier leaves, in pale greyish green. The pale stems are branching and bear the white flowers, with their bladder-like calyces behind, at the tips from May to September. The flowers are up to 2cm (¾in) across. The plants will thrive in the poorest of soils and are available from all the usual outlets. Seed can be saved towards the end of the growing season and sown in gritty compost.

Stachys lanata *Lamb's ears.*

Stachys lanata Lamb's ears

Grown for its grey, felty leaves and stems, this evergreen native of Turkey and Iran does flower, too. Borne in tall spikes, the flowers are small and mauvish in colour, on stems of soft, furry grey like the leaves at the height of summer. The plants grow to 45cm (18in) tall. The stems are erect and branching. There is a dwarf, non-flowering variety too. They grow best in a well-drained site, but can tolerate sun or partial shade. Commonly available as plants, they may also be propagated by division in spring or autumn.

Silene maritima *Sea campion.*

Symphytum officinale *Comfrey.*

Symphytum officinale Comfrey

Native to Europe, from Britain to the Caucasus, the comfreys are a long-known and much-used group of plants. Their medicinal and culinary uses have all but disappeared now, but they are still in limited use as animal fodder and, in the garden, for home-made plant feed. For this, the leaves are picked or the whole plants pulled up and put into a dustbin or water butt, where they are covered with water and allowed to rot down. The resulting brown liquid is diluted 1 in 10 in water for use. However, as an ornamental plant, there are varieties which grow to anything from 30cm (1ft) to 1.2m (4ft) in height, with flowers of white, pink, red or blue. All enjoy a well-drained soil and can tolerate either full sun or light shade. They flower from late spring well into the summer and can be found readily in garden centres and nurseries.

Thalictrum delaveii Meadow rue

There are several species of meadow rue which have found a home in gardens. Probably most often used is *T. aquilegifolium* with, as the name suggests, leaves that look like those of the columbine or aquilegia, but *T. flavum*, the British native, is also in use, as is the smaller *T. minus* and the tall, dark-leaved *T. speciosum*. *T. delaveii* is a delicate-looking plant with loose sprays of flower through the summer months. Illustrated is the variety Hewitt's Double, with little pom-poms of double flowers rather than the more usual single, although both generally just look like a mass of stamens. They enjoy a sunny site and, despite their first appearance, are quite resistant to strong winds, but prefer a soil with some moisture and body to it. Available from many nurseries and some garden centres, the species can be grown from seed in spring, although the varieties will not come true this way.

Thalictrum delaveii *Meadow rue.*

Verbascum phoeniceum *Dark mullein.*

Verbascum phoeniceum **Dark mullein**

Sometimes labelled as *V. hybridum*, there are several named varieties of the dark or purple mullein, in colours ranging from cream to purple and including yellow and orange. They all grow to 1 to 1.2m (3 to 4ft) and bear long flower spikes throughout the summer above rosettes of dark green leaves. Preferring a sunny site, they grow successfully in well-drained soil and can be grown from root cuttings in winter. Closely related and worthy of mention is the taller, grey-leaved and bright yellow flowered *V. olympicum*, which enjoys similar growing conditions and is sometimes seen as a wild flower in Britain. Both are available in garden centres and nurseries everywhere and are good growers in a seaside garden.

Veronica spicata **Spiked speedwell**

Originating across Europe and Asia, including Britain, there are many speedwells, some of which make a nuisance of themselves in the lawn, but most make worthy garden plants, either in the rockery or the herbaceous border. *V. spicata* grows to 30 to 45cm (1 to 1½ft), with narrow, lanceolate leaves held up the length of the stem as far as the base of the narrow, feathery, flower spike. There are blue, pink and white varieties. Illustrated is the white form. They like a well-drained site in sun or light shade and are available from most garden centres. Established clumps can be lifted and divided in spring or autumn.

Veronica spicata *Spiked speedwell.*

Watsonia **hybrids Watsonia**

Related to their fellow South Africans, the crocosmias, watsonias also grow from corms, though they naturally grow in damper ground. There are many species and varieties, with flowers in red, mauve, pink, orange and white. Not fully hardy, if your garden is prone to frosts then plant them deep in a well-drained soil. However, once established, they should be successful in most coastal sites. Water well in the growing season and they will give a mass of sword-like foliage, from which rise flowering stems up to 1.2m (4ft) in height, bearing long spikes of bright, tubular blooms from late spring well into the summer. Not commonly available outside their native country, they can be found in specialist nurseries and are well worth the search. Once established, clumps can be lifted and divided every other year.

Watsonia *hybrids Watsonia.*

There are many more perennials which make excellent seaside garden plants. Included among these are the following.

Achillea	**Yarrow**	Various garden hybrids, in white, red, pink and yellow, heights from 30cm (1ft) to 1.3m (4ft) in summer and autumn.
Alstromeria	**Peruvian lily**	Up to 75cm (2½ft). Orchid-like flowers in summer.
Bergenia	**Elephant's ears**	Round, glossy leaves up to 25cm (10in) across. Pink flowers borne in short spikes in spring and summer.
Centaurea nigra	**Knapweed**	Similar to perennial cornflower, but with mauve flowers. Up to 35cm (14in).
Centaurium erythraea	**Centaury**	Sprays of small, starry, pink flowers with yellow centres are held high from July to September on this small, light green plant.
Centranthus ruber	**Red valerian**	Mainly known as a cottage garden plant, it also comes in pink and white. Grows well in dry conditions. Flowers from late spring to early autumn.
Cheiranthus cheiri	**Wallflower**	Perennial often grown as a biennial. Best clipped back fairly hard after flowering. Light green lanceolate leaves beneath clusters of fragrant flower in late spring and early summer. Colours from yellow to purple.
Chionodoxa forbesii	**Glory of the snow**	Spring bulbs bearing starry blue or blue and white flowers in sun or partial shade.
Cicohorium intybus	**Chicory**	Up to 1.3m (4ft) with bright blue flowers along upper stems in summer.
Corydalis lutea	**Yellow fumitory**	Small ferny plant. Leaves like those of the aquilegias, short panicles of bright yellow flowers from spring to autumn. Grows in sun or shade.
Crocus		Small spring or autumn bulbs (in fact corms). Flowers pink, mauve, white or yellow.
Crocosmia		Sword-like leaves. Nodding spikes of red or orange flowers in late summer.
Dianthus	**Carnation**	Grey-green stems and narrow foliage carry a profusion of colourful semi-double flowers in high summer.
Dierama	**Wandflower**	Up to 75cm (2½ft). Fine stems with nodding white or pink flowers on the ends in mid to late summer.
Digitalis	**Foxglove**	Purple, white, pink or yellow finger-sized, bell flowers in early summer.
Echinacea	**Cone flower**	Large mauve/pink daisies with cone-shaped, central boss. Late summer. Up to 1m (3ft).
Echinops	**Globe thistle**	Erect plant with often blue, round, spiky flower heads in summer and autumn.

Echium	**Bugloss**	British native with bright blue summer flowers, up to 1m (3ft) or Canary Island hybrid with light blue flowers up to 4m (13ft).
Geranium		Various species and varieties with flowers in pink, white, blue or near-black. Up to 75cm (2½ft).
Glaucium flavum	**Horned poppy**	There are annual, biennial and perennial forms of the horned poppy, in yellow orange or red. Summer flowers. Native of seaside locations. Named for the seed heads.
Grasses		Many and varied, from 20cm (8in) *Festuca glauca*, blue fescue to 2m (6½ft) *Stipa gigantea* and pampas grass.
Gypsophilla		The classic light and floaty white blossom on finely branching stems. Annual and perennial species are available.
Hyacinthoides non-scripta	**Bluebell**	British native. The garden variety is a Spanish cross. Can be blue, pink or white and will tolerate shade or full sun, on rich or poor soil.
Iris		Dwarf, spring-flowering bulbs and larger summer-flowering rhizomatous plants in various colours.
Jasione montana	**Sheep-bit**	Rockery or grassland plant. Low clumps of deep green, lanceolate leaves, almost leafless flower stems bearing scabious-like buttons of bright blue flowers through the summer.
Leucanthemum vulgare	**Ox-eye daisy**	Large daisies in summer on plants up to 60cm (2ft) tall.
Lewisia		Succulent leaves in basal rosette. Flowers in several colours, often striped. Rockery plant. Best planted on an angle in wet climate.
Lotus corniculatus	**Bird's-foot trefoil**	Low and sprawling herbaceous plant with bright yellow, pea flowers from late spring to early autumn, especially if dead-headed often.
Lychnis coronaria		Basal evergreen rosette of grey foliage gives rise to branching, slender grey stems topped with many dark pink or white flowers in late summer.
Morina longifolia	**Whorl flower**	Thistle-like foliage, may be variegated, and tubular pink flowers like those of *Nicotiana*.
Narcissus	**Daffodils**	From dwarf 10cm (4in) to full-size 60cm (2ft). Yellow trumpeted flowers in spring.
Pelargonium	**Geranium**	Non-hardy, succulent-stemmed, leaves in mid-green or several variegations, flowers in white, red, orange or pink. Long flowering.
Penstemon		Semi-evergreen, upright plant. Mid-green lanceolate leaves topped by spires of tubular red, pink or white flowers in early to mid summer.

Physostegia virginiana	**Obedient plant**	Erect plant to 60cm (2ft). Lance-shaped leaves. Small pink or white flowers in tight panicles, mid to late summer.
Polygonum	**Knotweed**	Several types for sun, shade and even in the pond. Ovate leaves and tight oblong panicles of pink flowers through the summer.
Pulmonaria	**Lungwort**	Ovate leaves spotted with white. Red, pink, white or blue flowers in late spring and early summer.
Pulsatilla vulgaris	**Pasque flower**	Rockery plant. Hairy leaves and stems, purple, white or red flowers with hairy backs in late spring.
Ononis repens	**Rest-harrow**	For the rockery or wall. Small, hairy leaves, small, pink pea flowers July to September.
Scabious		Many and varied, from all over the world, but flower shape always distinctive – many tiny florets surrounded by larger petals. Blue, red or purple flowers through summer and early autumn.
Sempervivum	**Houseleek**	Succulent, rosette-forming, evergreen for the rockery or wall. Leaves green or reddish, flowers on short stems, greenish yellow to red.
Silene dioica	**Red campion**	Very tolerant hairy-stemmed plant. Pink flowers, single or double, April to September. Prefers some shade.
Strelitzia	**Bird of paradise**	Frost-tender. Banana-like leaves. Large orange and purple flowers on thick stems in summer. Up to 2m (6½ft).
Tradescantia	**Spiderwort**	Clump-former up to 60cm (2ft). Lanceolate leaves clasp the stem. Three petalled flowers in purple or white through the summer.
Tulips		Hundreds of varieties and species now in garden use, from 15cm (6in) to 60cm (2ft). Many colours and flower types. All flower in spring.
Zantedeschia aethiopica	**Arum lily**	Evergreen in warm climate. Large, narrowly heart-shaped leaves in dark green and broad white spathes surrounding yellow columnar spadix in summer.

CHAPTER 6

Shrubs

Shrubs are the woody plants that give structure and form to the beds and borders of the garden. They also provide hedging and shelter from wind and weather. They can be used to interrupt views so that the whole plot cannot be seen at once and the viewer is enticed into the garden to explore. They can be frost-hardy or tender, although this is of less importance in many coastal gardens than further inland, where frost is more of a problem. Tender shrubs, like tender perennials, can be rendered more frost-tolerant by planting them in a drier soil and mulching with a dry medium such as gravel or pebbles, making them ideal for the coastal garden. If your soil is not naturally dry, then a generous helping of sand or grit dug in when planting will help. This, combined with the milder coastal climate, will allow you to grow shrubs that would not be possible just a few miles inland. To be certain, however, it is always a good policy to take a few cuttings each season. When rooted, if they are not required in your own garden, they can always be given to friends or relatives.

Shrubs may be deciduous or evergreen. In these days of easy living and of maintaining maximum interest in the garden for minimum effort, evergreens are increasingly popular – with the possible exception of conifers and heathers, which were so fashionable in the 1960s and the 1970s that now they have gone to the opposite extreme in acceptability and few like to admit them into the garden. In moderation, however, both groups are useful and there are so many varieties that you can hardly fail to find something attractive among them. And not all evergreens are conifers or heathers – there are many others to choose from, from the periwinkles through lavender and rosemary to lilac and holly, to name just a few.

But the fact that a plant is deciduous does not mean that it has no value in the garden, even one that aims to maintain maximum interest all year. Many deciduous shrubs have an attractive bark, bright spring foliage, colourful autumn leaves and flowers and berries as well. Interest, with these, is maintained by variety, not the constancy of the evergreens. Again, examples abound, from the white-stemmed blackberry, through the dogwoods and willows to forsythia and fuchsias. Even after you have considered the stems and the leaves, these plants have more to offer. They often have bright or interesting fruit in late summer or autumn, such as the round, black 2 or 3cm (1in)-diameter hips of the burnet rose or the soft, grape-like fruits of the fuchsia. And preceding these there are the flowers, which are often as bright and abundant as those of the herbaceous plants that surround them in the border, although individually they may be less long-lasting.

Planted in their dormant phase, when they have no leaves through which moisture transpires, deciduous shrubs establish quickly, although they can also be planted when actively growing, as long as they are watered in well and kept watered until they are established. They are highly adaptable and extremely useful, providing the main winter interest in the form of permanent shapes in the garden. And with the careful choice of specimens, flowers and scents can be had every month of the year, even in temperate zones.

Aloe arborescens Aloe

This is one of the larger aloes and prefers full sun, while many of the smaller ones like some shade. Spreading up to 2m (6ft), the flower spikes will reach up at least as high when mature. Looking like a succulent-leaved cross between a yucca and its fellow South African kniphofia, this evergreen is

Aloe arborescens *Aloe.*

one of the few aloes which can be fully frost-hardy, although only if it does not sit in wet soil. Like the small rockery lewisias, it is best planted on an angle so that water does not sit in its crown in cold weather. Having achieved that, it will tolerate temperate climates, as proved by examples growing happily on top of Table Mountain. A very exotic plant for the coastal garden, it bears red or orange flowers in tall spikes from late winter into spring above rosettes of thick, tooth-edged leaves. Available from specialist nurseries and from garden centres in areas of the world where it is commonly grown, it can be propagated from offsets which can be cut away in warm weather and potted up to grow on in a sharply drained compost mixture.

Azalea.

Azalea
Part of the rhododendron group of ericaceous (acid-loving) shrubs from China and the Himalayas, confusingly, the azaleas are not all fully deciduous, just as the rhododendrons are not all evergreen. There are subtle differences in the leaves of the two groups. However, generally, the azaleas are thinner-leaved and deciduous, while the rhododendrons are thicker leaved and evergreen and the rhododendrons tend to bear their flowers in well-defined, rounded bunches while the azaleas tend to spread theirs more loosely. The semi-evergreen azaleas are the non-hardy, Japanese ones which are often grown as greenhouse and conservatory plants, while the deciduous ones are hardy and used in the garden. Flowers are borne through late April to June or sometimes later and can be found in colours ranging from white through yellows and pinks to red and orange. In autumn the foliage turns to bright oranges and copper colours before being shed. Plants are readily available, but propagation is not easy for the amateur. Layering can be done but may take up to two years to root. Acid soil is essential and some shelter is preferred, although not vital.

Berberis darwinii *Barberry.*

Berberis darwinii Barberry
There are members of the *Berberis* family from just about all over the world, including the United Kingdom, but *B. darwinii* comes from Chile. There are evergreen and deciduous varieties, the deciduous ones giving good autumn colour while the evergreens hold small, dark green leaves throughout the year. The flowers are small and bell-shaped, in

yellow or orange and borne profusely for several weeks in spring, to be followed by purple berries in late summer and autumn. *B. darwinii* grows to 2.5m (8ft), with a similar spread and its tiny, holly-like leaves are evergreen, among strong thorns which make it a good hedging plant. Any good garden soil will do, in sun or partial shade. Plants are readily available from the usual sources. Cuttings may be taken in summer or low stems can be layered, when they will root in a few months, ready to be cut away from the parent and planted separately.

Buddleia davidii *Butterfly bush.*

Buddleia davidii Butterfly bush

There are two other varieties of buddleia, *B. alternifolia*, which holds its mauve flowers in small bunches between the leaves on long, drooping branches and *B. globosa*, which has bunches of small, bright yellow spheres of flower at the ends of its branches. Both are interesting plants and well worth growing, but the classic buddleia is the *davidii* form, with its tapering racemes of purple, mauve, white or almost red flowers, with a honey scent, between July and September. These racemes are up to 30cm (1ft) long and borne profusely on arching stems, above soft, grey-green leaves. The plants should be pruned hard in autumn to prevent wind-rock, as they are shallow-rooted, and then again in spring to ensure good, young growth which will have plenty of flower. Without pruning, it will grow to 3m (9ft) or more, though its open habit ensures that it will not shade out those plants growing under it. Easily grown from cuttings of mature or semi-ripe wood, these hardy, deciduous plants are also readily available from nurseries and garden centres.

Callistemon rigidus *Bottlebrush bush.*

Callistemon rigidus Bottlebrush bush

These Australian bushes like plenty of sun and a fertile but well-drained soil. They are evergreen, with small, stiff leaves on arching stems and are hardy enough to grow in coastal gardens in most parts of the world. If your area is prone to very hard frosts, however, it may be wise to take cuttings or protect the plants in cold weather. The spectacular, red bottlebrush flowers are borne from July to October. Plants are increasingly easily available from garden centres and nurseries, but semi-ripe cuttings can be taken in summer or seed can be sown in autumn or spring, preferably under glass.

Camellia japonica *Camellia.*

Camellia japonica Camellia

Like the rhododendrons, which come from the same part of the world, the camellias are acid-lovers, as far as soil is concerned. There are numerous varieties, with flower types from single to fully double and colours from white through pink to deep red. A sheltered position and semi-shade are advised by many writers, but the plants will tolerate and even enjoy an open, sunny site. What does spoil them is hard frost while the flowers are on the plant. Like the magnolias, it turns the flowers brown and they are lost for that year. If frosted while the flowers are in bud, the flowers drop off and no more will be produced until next season. Easily found in nurseries and garden centres, they may be propagated from hardwood cuttings taken in autumn and potted in a sharply drained compost mix.

Cistus ladanifer *Rock rose.*

Chaenomeles *Japanese quince.*

Chaenomeles **Japanese quince**

Originating from China and Japan, the Japanese quince is closely related to the edible quince and also produces 3cm (1¼in) round fruits. But these tough shrubs, up to 2m (6ft) or more in height, are grown for their flowers, borne from March to May. Rose-like, cupped blossoms up to 3cm across, in colours from rose-tinted white through pink and orange to deepest red, often with prominent yellow stamens and sometimes with semi-double flowers, provide a prolific splash of colour against the dark stems in spring before the leaves open. Readily available from all the usual sources, they can also be propagated from 10cm (4in) heeled cuttings in late summer. They grow well in any aspect, doing particularly well against a wall or fence.

Cistus ladanifer **Rock rose**

These Mediterranean sun-lovers with their light green to grey-green foliage are excellent seaside plants with their ability to thrive in poor soils and strong winds. They enjoy full sun, but dislike being transplanted. Pruning should be kept light and restricted to when the showy yellow or white flowers have ceased to come. Most varieties flower in early to midsummer, some continuing into September, the flowers up to 7cm (3in) across. Not as common in garden centres as it was a few years ago, it is still to be found with a little effort and can be propagated from semi-ripe cuttings in late summer or from seed in autumn.

Cornus alba *Dogwood.*

Cornus alba Dogwood

The *Cornus* family contains many useful garden trees and shrubs, but *C. alba*, the red-barked dogwood, is the species that is native to Europe and Asia, including Britain. In the garden it is grown primarily for its decorative bark in winter, although the flattened heads of white flowers in spring and the whitish berries in late summer and autumn are also part of its attraction, along with the yellow autumn foliage and the rich yellowish tones of the spring leaf buds. Leaves are naturally a mid-green, but there are variegated varieties too. To maintain good bark colour, the shrub should be cut back hard every three years or so, in early spring. Readily available from garden centres and nurseries, it grows to a maximum height and spread of 3m (10ft), although it is often kept to 1.5 to 2m (4 to 6ft) in the garden. A tolerant plant, it will grow in any good garden soil, in sun or shade. Cuttings can be taken from semi-ripe wood in late summer and grown on in the ground or in pots of well-drained compost.

Erica Heather

There are so many members of the heather family, from all over the world, that only a small proportion of those native even in the same hemisphere are in common garden use. However, there is no good reason for this since most make good garden subjects and some, especially those of southern Africa, are truly spectacular in full flower. All will grow well in coastal conditions and there are examples that will tolerate just about any soil type you care to think of. They benefit from clipping back lightly after flowering to maintain a bushy habit, although they can be left to go woody and trained into small trees, their woody stems making ideal bonsai subjects. Slowly regaining popularity now, they were overused in the 1960s and 1970s to the point where many refused to entertain the thought of them, but with careful use they can make a worthwhile addition to any garden. The more exotic varieties can take some effort to find, but the common ones are readily available from all the usual places. They are generally evergreen, but can flower in any season, depending on the variety.

Erica *Heather.*

Euonymus fortunei *Euonymus.*

Euonymus fortunei Euonymus

This evergreen shrub, of which there are many varieties in varying shapes, sizes and leaf colours, is grown mainly as a foliage plant. The flowers are white and inconspicuous, borne in summer. Different varieties can grow to anything from 10cm (4in) to 1.2m (4ft) and fill just about any spot you wish with a splash of evergreen colour, though the larger *Euonymus japonica* is more useful as a hedge, as it is more upright and stiffer in habit, as well as being larger. Grow in full sun or light shade, in any good garden soil. Easily available from all the usual sources, it can also be propagated from semi-ripe cuttings in late summer or autumn.

Exochorda macrantha *Pearl bush.*

Exochorda macrantha Pearl bush

These deciduous Chinese bushes are almost entirely covered in 5cm (2in) white blooms for a few weeks in late spring, rivalling the best of the azaleas and the rhododendrons, although they are not as strictly ericaceous as those shrubs. A compact mound of drooping branches is formed by this garden cross, up to just 1.5m (5ft) tall. It prefers an open, sunny site, with well-drained soil. Not the most popular shrub in the list, it is available from nurseries and can be propagated by semi-ripe cuttings in late summer and autumn. These should be potted under glass and planted out in the following spring.

Fatsia japonica *Castor-oil plant.*

Fatsia japonica Castor-oil plant

This exotic-looking, Japanese bush, with its large, glossy, palmate leaves up to 45cm (18in) across, looks as if it belongs in the jungle but is, in fact, fully hardy. It can grow to a height and spread of 3m (10ft) and flowers profusely in autumn. Particularly successful in seaside gardens, it prefers some light shade but is tolerant of most soils. It is readily available to buy, but can also be grown from seed, sown in pots in spring or from autumn cuttings of semi-ripe wood.

Forsythia intermedia *Forsythia*.

Fuchsia *Fuchsia*.

Fuchsia *Fuchsia*

There are several species of *Fuchsia*, native to New Zealand and South America and literally hundreds of garden varieties, with flowers varying enormously in size and colour. All are deciduous and many are non-hardy, except in frost-free areas. Some, however, have naturalized in the hedges of Cornwall, in southern England. They will flower copiously from midsummer to late autumn, a non-stop spectacle of colour in full sun or partial shade, as long as they have a fairly rich and moisture-retentive soil. Cuttings could hardly be easier to root, in compost or even in a jar of water from non-flowering shoot tips, and plants are available everywhere.

Forsythia intermedia Forsythia

The masses of yellow flowers, borne on the leafless stems of this hardy, deciduous shrub in spring brighten many a garden while the daffodils and tulips flower beneath. There are several varieties with slightly different flower sizes and colour intensities, but all are yellow and cross-shaped and are followed by mid-green leaves through the summer. Pruning should not be done to excess, taking out only those branches which have flowered, after flowering is over. The bush will thrive in sun or light shade, in any good garden soil. Plants are readily available from all the usual sources, but cuttings are easily rooted in autumn or low shoots may be layered.

Hebe *Hebe*.

Hebe *Hebe*

Another New Zealander which has been taken to by gardeners in a big way, these evergreen shrubs have been developed into a range of sizes, leaf-sizes and colours as well as different flower colours. The last can be white, pink, purple, red or blue and carried from July to October on bushes from 15cm (6in) to 2m (6ft) tall. The bushes tend to be dense, although not too stiff in habit. Good for coastal planting, they enjoy well-drained soil in a sunny or lightly shaded spot. Like the fuchsias, non-flowering shoot tips up to 7cm (3in) long can easily serve as cuttings in summer, although plants are easily available.

Hibiscus rosa-sinensis *Hibiscus.*

Hibiscus rosa-sinensis **Hibiscus**

Usually grown as greenhouse or conservatory plants in Britain, in frost-free environments this woody, evergreen shrub with glossy, dark green leaves can reach a height of 3m (10ft), although it is often used as a hedging plant in places where it can grow outside. This includes temperate zones on the coast, where frost is not a problem. The large red flowers, up to 10cm (4in) across, are borne over a long period, starting in spring and going through to autumn, the main flush being in summer. Not easy to grow from cuttings, plants can be bought from nurseries and garden centres, but the hardier, deciduous *H. syriacus* is more commonly available in temperate areas for garden use and comes in several flower colours.

Hippophae rhamnoides *Sea buckthorn.*

Hippophae rhamnoides **Sea buckthorn**

Immune to wind, drought and salty air, this deciduous, grey-leaved bush is ideal for making a hedge in a seaside garden. Native to Britain and western Europe, its dense, spiny growth is tolerant of hard pruning, but left to its own devices it will grow to 6m (20ft). Tiny, white, spring flowers are followed by masses of bright orange berries that last from late summer through the winter, as long as you have both male and female plants. Not particularly common in garden centres or nurseries, it can be found with a little effort and, once obtained, is easily propagated by soft-wood cuttings in late summer, layering low shoots in autumn or sowing seed in autumn or spring.

Hypericum calycinum **Rose of Sharon**

This low-growing, dense shrub with its almost glossy, oval leaves is smothered in bright yellow flowers from early summer to autumn. It will grow in sun or light shade, in any good garden soil, as long as it is not waterlogged. It grows to just 45cm (1½ft) tall, but spreads to cover a great area of ground if allowed to do so. There are similar varieties which grow taller and more upright, if that is

Hypericum calycinum *Rose of Sharon.*

what you desire, or smaller ones for the rockery. There are also herbaceous perennials in the same family, including the British native St John's wort. Easily available from the usual sources, this plant is also easy to propagate by shoot-tip cuttings in the same way as the hebes and the fuchsias.

Kerria japonica *Jew's mallow.*

Kerria japonica **Jew's mallow**
This hardy and tolerant, deciduous, green-stemmed shrub is packed with little 2 to 3cm (1in) yellow balls of petals through April and May, then intermittently flowers during the summer. The stems are somewhat lax if allowed to grow long, but it responds well to pruning. Grows to 2.5m (8ft) if not pruned. The usual garden form is the double-flowered 'Pleniflora' variety. It will tolerate any good garden soil, in sun or light shade, and can be readily bought from garden centres and propagates easily from summer cuttings of softwood or by division in autumn.

Lavatera cachemiriana *Tree mallow.*

Lavandula spica **Lavender**
A group of small, fragrant shrubs whose grey-green leaves are borne densely on semi-ripe stems above old wood. Flowers are in tones of mauve and purple, carried high on thin stems and often visited by bees. Popularly cut and dried to use indoors, lavender needs a sunny, well-drained site. It is best trimmed lightly after flowering. Do not cut back into old wood. Easily available from the usual sources, it can be easily propagated by semi-ripe cuttings in summer. Makes an excellent low hedge for the edges of a path.

Lavatera cachemiriana **Tree mallow**
Much more commonly grown than the annual and herbaceous perennial mallows, the tree mallow is a soft-wooded shrub that will attain a height of 2.5m (8ft) if allowed to, but is more often seen at half that

Lavandula spica *Lavender.*

Leucospermum cordifolium *Pincushion bush.*

size. The branches tend to be rather brittle at the bases and to snap off when old, and so it is best treated as you would the hybrid roses and cut down fairly hard in autumn. It will then send up fresh shoots in spring. These are clothed intermittently with soft, greyish-green, felty leaves which are lobed in the same way as the sycamores and the abutilons. White, pink or mauve trumpet flowers, 5cm (2in) across, are borne in abundance from July to September. Will grow in any good garden soil, but prefers an open site. Available at garden centres and nurseries everywhere, it is also easily raised from cuttings in spring or summer.

Leucospermum cordifolium **Pincushion bush**
One of dozens of South African proteas which have found homes in gardens in that part of the world and are slowly gaining in popularity elsewhere for

their spectacular blooms, the pincushion bush needs a sunny position and well-drained soil to give of its best and a coastal site is ideal for this; although tolerant of wind, it is not entirely frost-hardy. The long, elliptic, dark green leaves are evergreen and densely held on bushes that can reach 1.2m (4ft) in height. Flowers up to 7.5cm (3in) across are carried profusely at the tips of the branches through the summer. Can be found in specialist nurseries, but it is not easy to propagate vegetatively; it can be sown as seed, under glass, in spring.

Olearia haastii **Daisy bush**
This native of New Zealand is one of those plants that is always quoted when the question is asked, what plants will grow well in a seaside garden? Disliking frost, but tolerant of strong wind, salty or polluted air and poor soil, it prefers a sunny site and good drainage. *O. haastii* grows to 2m (6ft) tall. The

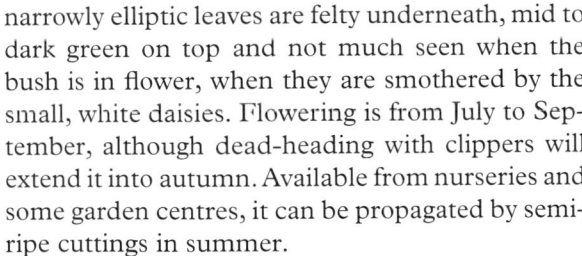

Olearia haastii *Daisy bush.*

Phlomis fruticosa *Jerusalem sage.*

narrowly elliptic leaves are felty underneath, mid to dark green on top and not much seen when the bush is in flower, when they are smothered by the small, white daisies. Flowering is from July to September, although dead-heading with clippers will extend it into autumn. Available from nurseries and some garden centres, it can be propagated by semi-ripe cuttings in summer.

Phlomis fruticosa Jerusalem sage

Who needs flowers when you have foliage like this, densely clothing a bush that will reach a height of just 1m (3ft), but spread up to twice that distance? Still, flowers there are. Yellow, hook-shaped ones about 2.5cm (1in) long, held in whorls around the stems, between the grey-green, velvety leaves for several weeks at the height of summer. An ever-green from the eastern Mediterranean, the Jerusalem sage dislikes frost, but enjoys a sunny spot in well-drained soil, preferably with some protection from cold winds. Not as popular as it might be, it is still available from most nurseries and some garden centres and can be propagated from semi-ripe cuttings in summer or seed under glass in spring.

Phormium tenax New Zealand flax

Mainly grown for its tufts of stiff, sword-shaped, dark green leaves, some varieties having variegations of cream or bronze and there is one with entirely bronze leaves. *P. tenax* is an evergreen which may reach a height of 3m (10ft) and mature specimens will bear panicles of tubular flowers on short, blue-green stems in summer. Commonly

Phormium tenax *New Zealand flax.*

Photinia fraseri *'Red Robin'.*

available in nurseries and garden centres, it much resembles the cordylines, but is hardier, with thicker leaves. Enjoys a sunny position and moist but well-drained soil. Can be propagated by division in spring or from seed.

Photinia fraseri 'Red Robin'

This hybrid was produced less than fifty years ago, but has gained great popularity for its striking, red, young foliage in spring. Unlike the pieris, which also bears red leaves on its shoot tips and is another worthwhile plant for the garden, this one does not need an acid soil, though it does enjoy a sunny site. It will grow to 2.5m (8ft) and the flaming red shoot tips mature to copper before turning deep green. Older growth may be cut back to maintain size and encourage new young shoots next spring. Semi-

ripe cuttings can be potted in summer, in a sharply drained compost mix. The plants are readily available from the usual sources. A good choice for the seaside garden.

Phyllostachys aurea Bamboo

There are many bamboos available, of all heights and in many stem-colours, leaf colours and variegations, some spreading and others clump-forming, but this is a good all-rounder for most gardens. The golden stems will reach 6 to 8m (20 to 25ft) if allowed to do so, but it is a clump-former, evergreen and frost-hardy. Leaves are mid-green, up to 15cm (6in) long and rustle in the wind as the stems wave against each other. Readily available from garden centres and nurseries, it can be propagated by division in spring.

Phyllostachys aurea *Bamboo.*

Potentilla fruticosa *Shrubby cinquefoil.*

Potentilla fruticosa Shrubby cinquefoil

Tiny, mid green leaves clothe this shrub for most of the year, although it is deciduous in all but the mildest of climates. Responding well to clipping, it forms a good hedge and is one of the most floriferous of the garden shrubs, bearing its 2.5cm (1in)-wide, flat flowers in colours from white through pale yellow to orange and red, from May until autumn. It will thrive in any reasonable soil, but prefers it well-drained; it can tolerate sun or partial shade. Many varieties are available from nurseries and garden centres. Plants can be propagated easily from semi-ripe cuttings in summer or by transplanting the self-sown seedlings that will undoubtedly appear beneath the plants.

Pyracantha coccinea Firethorn

Glossy, mid-green leaves clothe this tough and hardy plant all year, but offer no protection against the spines with which it is also well-endowed. A good plant for growing against a wall or fence, it can be clipped into whatever shape you wish, up to its maximum height of 3.5m (12ft). Bunches of small, white flowers are borne in summer, but are not nearly as showy as the berries which replace them, maturing to rich red, orange or yellow in autumn and staying on the plant for a long time – especially so with the orange and yellow ones, which are less popular with birds. Any reasonable soil will do, including chalky ground, in sun or light shade. Plants are readily available from all the usual sources and can be grown from semi-ripe cuttings in summer. Seed can also be sown in spring.

Pyracantha coccinea *Firethorn.*

Santolina chamaecyparissus *Cotton lavender.*

Senecio compactus *Senecio.*

Santolina chamaecyparissus Cotton lavender

There are several varieties of cotton lavender, with green or grey foliage and flowers from 1 to 2.5cm (½ to 1in) across, but all are evergreen, with finely divided leaves growing from stems that can go woody if the plant is not cut back after flowering, which takes place from June to August. The flowers are yellow, on plants that can reach 0.7 to 1m (2 to 3ft) in height, though some varieties stay much shorter than this. Prefers a sunny, well-drained site. Plants are available from nurseries and garden centres; 5 to 7cm (2 to 3in) cuttings can be rooted in sharply drained compost in summer.

Senecio compactus Senecio

The most commonly grown shrubby senecio is *S. greyi*, with its characteristic grey, downy, young foliage and yellow daisy flowers in high summer. *S. compactus* is also well worth growing, however. It has similar flowers, over the same time period, and a similar habit and size – up to 1m (3ft) tall by 1m across – but its leaves are different. They have toothed edges, rather than the smooth ones of *S. greyi* and tend to show up those edges more prominently with their white hairs. Both plants prefer a sunny, well-drained position, although they do not mind what kind of soil they are in and nor do they mind the wind and salt spray of a seaside garden. While *S. greyi* is commonly available, *S. compactus* may take rather more finding, but it is well worth the trouble. Cuttings 10cm (4in) long can be taken in summer and rooted under glass.

Ulex europaeus *Common gorse.*

Ulex europaeus **Common gorse**

Its long season of interest is just one of the attributes which commends gorse to the gardener. Although the native plant grows up to 2.7m (8ft), there is a dwarf variety which attains only half that height and can be clipped to whatever size is required, forming a dense hedge of tiny, mid-green leaves on spiny stems. Long trusses of rich yellow, fragrant flowers are borne heavily from February to the end of April and more will come throughout the year, especially if the bush is clipped in early summer. On mature plants, the spines form the only foliage, although normal leaves are evident on young growth. Gorse will tolerate almost any conditions, although it dislikes chalky soils. It is available from nurseries and is easily propagated from seed, which should be scarified before being sown in spring or autumn. It will also grow from semi-ripe cuttings, although you will need gloves to pot them up.

Viburnum juddii *Viburnum.*

Viburnum juddii **Viburnum**

There are many viburnums, from temperate regions all across the northern hemisphere, including Britain. *V. juddii* is a cross between the Korean *V. carlesii* and another species, to give the strongly fragrant spring flowers of *V. carlesii* with an improved leaf shape. It is a deciduous shrub which grows up to 1m (3ft) tall. Its pink-flushed, white flowers are borne from mid to late spring, in well-defined clusters up to 7.5cm (3in) across. The dark, ovate leaves turn maroon in autumn, before dropping. Any good garden soil will suffice, but it will not thrive in thin, poor ground. A little shelter from cold winds will benefit the flowers, as will a west-facing position if frost is a problem in your garden. Plants are available from garden centres and nurseries and can be propagated from heeled cuttings of softwood lateral shoots in summer. These require a little bottom-heat to encourage rooting. Layering in autumn also works with the viburnums. New plants created in this way require about a year to root before they can be separated from the parent.

Vinca major *Periwinkle.*

Yucca filamentosa *Yucca.*

April to September, with the main flush in May or June. They are up to 2.5cm (1in) across on plants that reach only about 20 to 25cm (8 to 10in) high but will scramble for several feet along the ground or through other plants. Commonly available from all the usual sources, they can also be easily layered by pegging down a shoot, especially at a leaf node. *V. minor* is very similar but physically smaller and just as useful in the garden.

Yucca filamentosa **Yucca**
A plant for those who want to make a statement, the yucca should be given room for you to enjoy the impact of its dark green, sword-like leaves and huge, white flower heads, up to 3m (10ft) tall. Flower spikes can open at any time from July to October on this evergreen perennial. Originating from Mexico and the southern United States, it requires a well-drained soil and enjoys full sun, but it can thrive in partial shade. Available from garden centres, it can be propagated by removing and potting up rooted offsets from around its base in spring.

Vinca major **Periwinkle**
Native to Europe and Britain, the periwinkle is a loose scrambler, rather than a well-defined, shrubby plant, but it creates a good, dense mass of evergreen foliage if given room to do so. The pointed leaves are naturally glossy and mid-green, but there are also variegated varieties available for garden use. Hardy and adaptable, it will grow in sun or shade, in moist or dry ground. The blue or mauve flowers are displayed prominently from

Ceanothus *California lilac*

There are many more shrubs which will suit a seaside garden, some of which are listed below.

Artemesia	**Wormwood**	Silver-leaved, soft shrubs which will tolerate sun or shade.
Atriplex halimus	**Tree purslane**	Semi-evergreen, bushy, rarely flowers. Silver-grey leaves, 2m (6ft).
Buxus sempervivens	**Box**	Good hedging or topiary bush. Will grow large if allowed to. Evergreen.
Caryopteris		Deciduous. Pale foliage. Blue flowers, late summer and autumn.
Ceanothus	**California lilac**	Several garden varieties, from small to large, evergreen, flowers pale to dark blue, May to June.

Choisya	**Mexican orange blossom**	Evergreen shrub. Green or yellow foliage, white flowers. Fragrant.
Cortaderia selloana	**Pampas grass**	Large, evergreen clump-former with 30 to 60cm (1 to 2ft) heads of whitish flowers, replaced by similar-looking seed which stay on all winter.
Eleagnus		Evergreen shrubs. Leaves green, yellowish, variegated or greyish. Good hedging plant on the coast.
Escallonia		Evergreen. Small, dark green, glossy foliage. Small pink or red tubular flowers in summer.
Genista	**Broom**	Green stems, tiny leaves, yellow or cream flowers in spring. Needs a little shelter from strong winds.
Griselinia littoralis	**Broadleaf**	Evergreen, upright. Good hedge for coastal areas. Leaves bright green or variegated. Yellowish flowers in late spring.
Hydrangea		Deciduous, tough plant. 15cm (6in) heads of bloom, blue pink or white. Colour can be affected by soil pH in some types.
Leycesteria formosa	**Himalayan honeysuckle**	Deciduous. Blue-green shoots, dark green leaves. Red bracts and white flowers, followed by purple fruit.
Ligustrum lucidum	**Chinese privet**	Related to the British native *L. vulgare*, but more reliably evergreen. Green or yellowish leaves. Small conical clusters of white flowers in late spring.
Mahonia		Several types. Evergreen, spiky foliage sometimes turns red in early spring. Yellow flowers in clusters in spring.
Philadelphus coronarius	**Mock orange**	Deciduous. Green, yellow-green or variegated leaves. White flowers, highly fragrant, in summer.
Pittosporum crassifolium	**Karo**	Evergreen large shrub. Leaves oblong, dark green above, felted grey beneath. Small, fragrant reddish flowers in clusters in spring.
Rhododendron		Mostly evergreen but some deciduous. Large, glossy leaves, some types felted or red beneath. Clusters of trumpet flowers in spring. Many colours and sizes. For acid soil.
Rosa pimpinellifolia	**Burnet rose**	British native bush. Grows on the coast. Compact habit. White flowers in summer, large, round, black hips in autumn.
Rosemarinus officinalis	**Rosemary**	Evergreen fragrant shrub. Tiny dark green leaves on greyish stems. Blue flowers in late summer.
Ruscus aculeatus	**Butcher's broom**	Small, spiky bush for a shady spot. Tiny but fascinating flowers in spring followed by little red berries.
Spartium junceum	**Spanish broom**	Almost leafless, green stems, bright yellow flowers in summer. Like *Genista* but larger flowers.
Thyme		Group of several low-growing evergreen shrubs. Includes many carpeters. Several leaf colours and sizes. Pink or white flowers in summer.

CHAPTER 7

Trees and Climbers

While annuals and herbaceous perennials give bulk and shrubs give structure to a garden, it is trees and climbers that we turn to when we need height. Climbers can take the eye upwards, covering fences, hedges, arches, pergolas or walls as well as climbing through trees, while trees give the garden a sense of scale, standing free and proud either at the boundaries or in the middle of lawns or borders. Trees lend shelter and a sense of enclosure that nothing else can. One can sit under a tree and feel cosy, even in the open. A tree creates its own small environment, attracting birds, insects and other wildlife into the garden.

Trees are best planted in autumn, though the less hardy types may be planted in spring and kept well watered for their first season until they have had time to establish a good root system. Staking is best done low, with the stake driven in at an angle so that it stabilizes the base of the tree, while allowing the top to firm up and adapt to the conditions of the site.

There are trees for every garden, from dwarf cherries and miniature weeping pussy-willows to huge pines, oaks and chestnuts. Like shrubs, they can be deciduous or evergreen, dense or open. They can be hardy or tender, need shelter or enjoy an open site. Every situation will require something different, but there are sufficient species and varieties to suit any aspect of any garden. And, it is true to say that, whether open or sheltered, formal or informal, every garden should have at least one tree. You must, though, select carefully for the site you have in mind. Never use a tree that is too large or too dense, close to the house. Always check the growth rate and the final size of any tree before purchase and never place it where its final root run – often roughly the same size as the canopy above ground – could impinge on any building, road or other important structure. Having said that, trees are to be enjoyed throughout the year. Like shrubs, many have attractive bark, good autumn colour, flowers and fruits in the relevant season and, with careful choice, the season of interest can be extensive.

Nevertheless, trees can sometimes be made to look interesting for even longer by the judicious use of climbers scrambling up through them. The apples, plums and cherries, for example, give good blossom in spring, fruit and leaf colour in autumn, but are fairly undistinguished through the summer. This can be helped by training a summer-flowering clematis or some other climber through them.

Like trees, climbers come in many sizes and the choice of which to use must depend, at least partly, on the size of the area to be covered. It is no good using a Russian vine to cover a small arch in the garden or trying to persuade a sweet pea to cover a pergola. Climbers may be annual or perennial, evergreen or deciduous, used for flower colour or leaf. Again, there are many choices and the seaside gardener enjoys a wider choice than many others because of the relatively mild conditions enjoyed in such a site, although some climbers will need careful positioning in order to survive the wilder weather sometimes experienced on the coast. Furthermore, the potential time span of interest in the garden is extensive, with ivy giving leaf colour all year and unusual berries in spring, while many climbers flower through the summer and some give spectacular autumn leaf colour. The clematis group can produce flowers from spring through to late autumn. While climbers demand a degree of care and attention, especially early in their lives, they repay it a hundredfold over time, hiding less attractive aspects of the garden and adding interest to boring walls and fences. And how could anyone have a garden without the scent of either honey-suckle or jasmine?

Albizia julibrissin *Silk tree.*

Albizia julibrissin Silk tree

These spectacular, small, deciduous trees, with their feathery, mid-green, acacia-like foliage and beautiful pink and white brushes of flower stamens, are not fully hardy when young and so should be grown under glass until they achieve a truly woody stem, if there is risk of frost in your location. But they are well worth the effort, flowering profusely from July to October in a sunny, well-drained site.

Arbutus unedo *Strawberry tree.*

Arbutus unedo Strawberry tree

A now rare native of Britain and south-western Europe, the strawberry tree makes an interesting garden specimen since it flowers and fruits at the same time. The small, white almost heather-like flowers are replaced by 1.5cm (½in) diameter round fruits which ripen gradually from green to red among glossy, dark green, evergreen leaves. The bark is a rich mid-brown, like that of the yew. The strawberry tree prefers a site with a little shelter from strong wind and, when young, from harsh frost. Any good garden soil will suffice.

Betula pendula *Silver birch.*

Betula pendula Silver birch

There are several species among the birches, all deciduous, and all well worth inclusion, if you have the space for a medium to large tree. Like the aspen, to which they are related, they have slender, mobile twigs which tend to move in the wind, lending another appeal to the garden. The silver birch can reach up to 33m (100ft), although usually it attains only half that. It will thrive in sun or semi-shade. Its canopy is open enough not to cast heavy shade and its trunk generally remains slender or can be multi-stemmed. The white main trunk and branches give way to reddish twigs clothed in light green leaves that turn yellow in autumn. Catkins are borne in April. One of the most popular of the north European native trees for garden use, it is highly adaptable and will tolerate a wide range of conditions. Small trees are freely available from nurseries and garden centres. Seed can be gathered and sown in winter, but the thin, whippy twigs are too slender to make useful cuttings.

Chamaecyparis lawsoniana *False cyprus.*

Chamaecyparis lawsoniana False cyprus
Native to the west coast of North America, Lawson's cyprus is a hardy, conical, evergreen conifer that grows up to 13m (40ft) in height. However, it has shown itself to be readily hybridized and there are numerous varieties now grown for the garden which reach anything from 45cm (18in) to 2m (6ft). The mid-green foliage is replaced in some varieties with pale green or golden yellow and the fruiting bodies are light grey, maturing to little brown cones barely 1cm (⅜in) across. These plants generally require some shelter from strong winds and prefer a moisture-retentive soil, but are good specimens for within the confines of a garden with an established windbreak. It is one of the parents of the much-maligned Leylandii. Plants are readily available from garden centres or can be produced from cuttings in late winter or spring. Strong new shoots about 10cm (4in) long should be taken with a heel and placed in a sharply drained potting compost mixture.

Cotinus coggygria *Smoke tree.*

Cotinus coggygria Smoke tree
This small, deciduous tree, native to southern Europe, adds interest to the garden for a large part of the year. Its round to ovate leaves are light green or dark bronze, according to the variety chosen, and colour to reds and golds in autumn, after the feathery inflorescences, which start to come out in midsummer, have fruited in great balls of red fluff up to 20cm (8in) across. It is these flowers and fruiting plumes that give the tree its name. It can be grown in any good garden soil, preferring a sunny position and a well-drained site. Saplings can be planted in autumn. Shoots can be layered or 10 to 12cm (4–5in) cuttings can be taken from lateral shoots in early autumn for rooting in a sharply drained medium.

Cupressus macrocarpa *Monterey cyprus.*

Eucalyptus *Eucalyptus.*

Cupressus macrocarpa Monterey cyprus

This vigorous, Californian evergreen can reach 16m (50ft) if allowed to do so, although it responds well to clipping. There are dark and pale varieties. All are columnar when immature, but spread and become flat-topped if allowed to mature. Young trees, or those kept clipped, form a good barrier hedge but can brown on the windward side if the wind is too cold for them. Like all conifers of this type, do not prune into old wood. Cones are red-brown, spherical, about 2 to 3cm (1in) in diameter and borne in clusters along the shoots; the leaves are aromatically fragrant when crushed. Plant in spring or autumn. Seedlings less than 60cm (2ft) high are the easiest to establish. They will tolerate any good garden soil, although young plants dislike the north wind. Cuttings 7 to 10cm (3 to 4in) long, with a heel, can be rooted in autumn in a sharply drained compost mix.

Eucalyptus Eucalyptus

These Australian evergreens are ever popular for their attractive bark, grey-green leaves and rapid growth in all kinds of situation. There are over 600 species and hybrids, varying enormously in mature height and spread, and so there is bound to be one to suit your garden. Smooth bark and an open canopy as well as colourful young foliage add to their attractions. They will tolerate most conditions, but dislike root disturbance, therefore young plants should be put in and securely staked. They are best planted in summer and watered well for the first season. In the first winter they may benefit from being surrounded by straw or bracken, but thereafter they should be hardy enough on their own. Seed does not mature until the year after flowering, but then can be sown in early spring under glass. Plant out seedlings at 15 to 20cm (6 to 8in) height.

Fagus sylvatica **Beech**

Like the hornbeam, which is broadly similar in appearance, the beech may be used as a specimen tree or as a hedging plant. The beech comes in natural green- or copper-leaved forms. Either can attain 33m (100ft) if allowed to mature, with a trunk girth of 2m (6ft) or more, but can equally be kept clipped to form a dense hedge. Although they are strictly deciduous, both plants retain their leaves, albeit brown and dead-looking after their golden autumn show, well into winter and so are suitable as part of a shelter belt. Any good garden soil is suitable, in sun or light shade, although it should be fairly deep. Bare-rooted plants are commonly sold in autumn from garden centres and nurseries and pencil-thick cuttings can be taken in late summer for rooting in a shady spot ready for transplanting a year or so later.

Fagus sylvatica *Beech.*

Garrya elliptica **Silk tassel tree**

Originating on the West Coast of the USA, this large shrub or small tree is grown primarily for its attractive, large catkins, which hang beyond the thick, evergreen, ovoid, glossy leaves in spring. The catkins may be up to 23cm (9in) long and are a yellowish grey colour. Plants are single-sex and it is the males that produce the larger catkins, although both male and female are available. They quickly achieve a height of up to 5m (15ft) and can spread to almost 3m (9ft). They dislike root disturbance and are best planted out when young as container-grown plants. They will tolerate sun or shade, in any well-drained soil, but they can benefit from a degree of shelter from cold winds. Cuttings can be taken in autumn, with a heel, from semi-ripe wood

Garrya elliptica *Silk tassel tree.*

and rooted in pots of sharply drained compost or long shoots can be layered in autumn, although they take up to two years to root in this way.

Gleditsia triacanthe **Pea tree/Honey locust tree**

One of the few examples of this genus whose flowers are at all significant, this small, hardy, deciduous North American tree has long, pinnate leaves of light green which turn golden yellow in autumn. The long, twisted seed pods stay on the tree all winter. It grows to a height of 6 to 10m (20 to 30ft), spreading its loose canopy up to 5m (15ft). The honey locust will grow in any good garden soil and can be planted as a young sapling at any time through autumn, winter or early spring, in frost-free weather. It is best to plant out two- or three-year-old specimens. These can be grown from seed, sown into pots in spring.

Gleditsia triacanthe *Pea tree/Honey locust tree.*

Ilex aquifolium **Holly**

There are far too many cultivated varieties of this popular garden tree or shrub to mention here. They come in natural green or several variegations, with yellow, cream or white edging to the spiny-edged, evergreen leaves. The main trunk matures from green to chocolate brown, remaining smooth as it ages and expands. Small, white flowers are borne close to the stem in May, turning to red berries by late autumn on female plants. The tree can grow up to 20m (60ft) in the wild, but can be clipped to any size and shape required in the garden. With its dense foliage, it provides a good windbreak when needed. It will grow in any good garden soil, but will not tolerate wet ground. It can thrive in sun or shade. Plants are readily available from nurseries and garden centres. Pencil-thick cuttings can be rooted easily in the warmer months.

Ilex aquifolium *Holly.*

Jacaranda mimosifolia *Jacaranda.*

Jacaranda mimosifolia Jacaranda

This spectacular tree is rarely grown in the northern hemisphere because it has a reputation for difficulty, but to see it in the Drakensberg mountains or as an avenue tree in Pretoria in South Africa is to be convinced that it is worth a try. Although young plants may be frost-tender, they are fully hardy by the time their trunks become woody. Fast growers, they can achieve a height of 12m (37ft) or more, with their finely-cut, ferny foliage smothered in mauve flowers in spring, if grown in a sunny position. They prefer a well-drained soil and can be propagated easily from seed, which are borne in flat, round pods, or from semi-ripe cuttings in spring.

Laburnum anagyroides *Laburnum tree.*

Laburnum anagyroides Laburnum tree

Also known as the golden chain tree, this deciduous native of southern Europe is a popular and hardy garden plant which can tolerate full sun or light shade and any soil that is not too wet. It can grow to 7m (22ft). The grey-green leaves are divided into three oval leaflets which are still sparse by the time the long, pendant clusters of yellow pea-like flowers open in late spring through to early summer. Not easy from cuttings, plants are readily available from garden centres and nurseries. They should be staked when young, and planted any time from autumn to spring.

Musa basjoo *Banana.*

Musa basjoo Banana

Most of the bananas, being of tropical origin, have no frost hardiness, but the variety Basjoo, from Japan, is sufficiently hardy to grow inland in Britain, if the false stem (made up of dead leaf-stalks from previous years) is kept protected with straw or bracken through the coldest months. This is not relevant in frost-free areas, of course. Here, it is evergreen, the leaves being up to 1.5m (5ft) long. Drooping, pale yellow flowers, if grown in a sufficiently sunny location, will be followed by greenish fruit. A height of 3 to 5m (10 to 15ft) can be attained. Plants are increasingly available through the usual sources.

Pinus montezumae *Mexican pine.*

Pyrus salicifolia pendula *Weeping willow-leaved pear.*

Pinus montezumae **Mexican pine**

One of many pines, several of which have similarly long, flexible needles, the Mexican pine has needles of greyish hue and cones up to 15cm (6in) long. It grows up to 16m (50ft) tall, when mature, with a rough-textured bark. A magnificent tree for the larger garden, like many pines it thrives in a seaside environment. Also good for coastal sites are the beach pine, *P. contorta* and the Corsican pine, *P. nigra maritima*. All these can be grown from seed, when the mature cones release them, or bought as young plants from nurseries. They all prefer good light, although most soil types will suffice. Water them well until established and they will reward you with evergreen growth that adds stature and majesty to your garden.

Pyrus salicifolia pendula **Weeping willow-leaved pear**

The weeping habit and narrow, silvery leaves of this little tree are sufficiently different to be worthwhile in the garden, even without the white spring blossom and autumn fruits. The pears are small and hard but still edible. Fully hardy, the pears need cross-pollination from another pear or an apple in order to fruit, but this tree is small enough, growing to just 7m (22ft) tall, to have two if you do not want to grow any other fruit trees. But several of the apples are highly decorative, too and not much work. The dense, weeping habit is ideal for children to play in, although the trunk and root system are strong enough to withstand strong winds, especially if the tree is staked when young, until it estab-

lishes itself. Autumn foliage is yellow. Plants are available from nurseries. Cuttings and seed are not reliable methods of propagation for this variety.

Sorbus aucuparia **Rowan**

Also known as the mountain ash, for the resemblance of its divided deciduous leaves to those of the ash, it is debated whether the rowan's name derives from its long association with witchcraft or from its copious, red, autumn berries. The finely segmented, mid-green leaves appear in April and are soon followed in May and June by flat panicles of white flowers which then turn to berries of red or orange. These are held through the autumn, when they look lovely among the yellowing foliage of the open crown. The tree will grow in almost any situation. Young plants are readily available from garden centres and nurseries. Bare-root saplings can be planted in autumn or winter, pot-grown ones at any time of year, as long as they are kept watered until they are established. Berries can be harvested or cuttings taken in autumn.

Sorbus aucuparia *Rowan.*

Spathodea campanulata **Flame tree**

For those whose gardens are truly frost-free, there are few more spectacular statements to be made than with this African evergreen. The deeply divided leaves have anything up to nineteen lobes and the tulip-shaped, flame-red flowers appear copiously in clusters through autumn to spring. Growing up to 17m (55ft) tall, it requires a fertile, well-drained soil and good light. Its wood is almost as light as balsa, but the broad root-base stabilizes it well in windy conditions. It will not flower when young, but, when it does, it is worth the wait. Propagation may be done from seed or semi-ripe cuttings in spring. Plants are available only from specialist nurseries except in its native Africa.

Spathodea campanulata *Flame tree.*

Tamarix tetrandra *Tamarisk.*

Tamarix tetrandra **Tamarisk**

The unique feathery effect of the tiny, grey-green leaves, combined with the plumes of tiny, pale pink flowers cannot be mistaken for anything else. Not nearly as delicate as it looks, the tamarisk is a favourite for exposed coastal gardens, where it will withstand all that the elements can throw at it. It likes a sunny site in well-drained soil and can tolerate quite severe pruning, which is best done after its flowering in May. Often used as a shrub, when it can be clipped to become quite dense, it forms a loose tree up to 4m (12ft) tall if allowed to grow unchecked. Very similar, but tending to be darker in both leaf and flower is *T. pentandra*, which flowers in August. There is a dark, purplish-flowered variety of this one, known as Rubra. Tamarisks are deciduous, but fully hardy. Readily available from nurseries and garden centres, they can also be grown from 30cm (1ft) hardwood cuttings taken in autumn and planted into dryish ground.

Taxus baccata *Yew.*

Taxus baccata **Yew**

Another native of Britain and northern Europe which can be clipped as a hedge or allowed to grow into a grand tree of anything up to 15m (50ft) in height. Unusually among the conifers, the yew will regrow from old wood and thus can be clipped as hard as necessary to achieve a desired effect. There are several commercially grown varieties, with prostrate or columnar habit and some with golden leaves, but the dark green-leaved native type is as good as any. Insignificant white flowers in spring are followed on female plants by fleshy, scarlet, cup-shaped fruits which contain poisonous seed. The evergreen, finely divided leaves give dense cover and, like the holly, the tree will grow in sun or shade. It will tolerate most conditions except poor drainage. Young plants are slow to grow until established. It will take ten years to reach 2m (6ft) from seed, which can be sown in autumn, in sharply drained compost or where it is to grow, although plants are readily available from the usual sources.

Bougainvillea × buttiana.

Bougainvillea × buttiana

Originating from Brazil, these woody-stemmed, scrambling, deciduous climbers need to be kept frost-free, which is why they are used as greenhouse or conservatory plants in temperate countries such as Britain, while being popular as garden plants in warmer regions, such as the Mediterranean area. Given good light and a mild climate, they are well worth growing and will rapidly clothe a wall or a pergola with their elliptic leaves and masses of showy bracts with the small white flowers at their centre. The basic type has purplish mauve bracts, but there are varieties with orange, red and white also. The bracts form flower-like structures about 3 to 4cm (1 to 1½in) across. Getting them to flower a second time can be difficult, but the trick is to treat them harshly: do not water them after flowering until they are drooping severely, then soak them well. The plant will climb to 5m (15ft), preferring a sunny position and well-drained soil. Cuttings are easily rooted in a mixture of sharp sand and compost. This can be done with semi-ripe wood in summer or with mature wood in winter, when it is best to use a little bottom heat to encourage rooting. Plants are readily available from nurseries and garden centres.

Bryonia dioica *Common bryony.*

Bryonia dioica **Common bryony**
A native of Britain and northern Europe, the common bryony is not used in the garden as much as it deserves. Climbing by means of tendrils, it reaches only 2 to 3m (6 to 9ft) tall, but has heart-shaped, glossy, mid-green leaves with small white flowers in summer that look a little like those of its much more vigorous fellow British native, old man's beard, the wild clematis. These are followed in late summer and autumn by shiny, bright, red berries. The leaves turn golden yellow in autumn. It makes an excellent contrast to some of the other climbers, with which it can be grown, such as sweet pea and hop. It is available commercially only from specialist nurseries, but can be rooted from cuttings or sown as seed. The berries should be collected in

autumn and the flesh stripped from them before sowing in a sharply drained compost mixture and leaving out over winter. The plant will tolerate sun or light shade and any good garden soil.

Campsis radicans *Trumpet vine.*

Campsis radicans **Trumpet vine**
Two varieties of trumpet vine are grown in the garden, one from China, the other from the USA. *C. radicans* is the American one, the main difference between the two being in the leaves, which have smooth undersides in the Chinese species. Deciduous, woody-stemmed root-climbers like ivy, the trumpet vines have large, mid-green leaves and produce bunches of large, red trumpet flowers up to 7.5cm (3in) long through late summer and autumn. Although fully hardy, they require some shelter from strong winds and a rich soil kept watered through the summer. Given that, they will grow to 10 to 12m (30 to 40ft) if required, but can be pruned hard in early spring before growth starts. Young plants should be cut back to within 15cm (6in) of ground level after planting to encourage basal shooting. Support on canes or something similar until the aerial roots begin to appear. Propagation can be by semi-ripe cuttings in summer or hardwood cuttings in winter. Additionally, seed can be sown in pots under glass in spring. Plants are available from garden centres.

Eccremocarpus scaber **Chilean glory vine**
These dainty-looking tendril climbers are often grown as annuals, although they are perennial. As the name suggests, they originate in South America and enjoy full sun and a well-drained soil. The

Eccremocarpus scaber *Chilean glory vine.*

iegations, twines and climbs up anything it can reach, although there are now trailing varieties which have been bred not to climb. But once the plant reaches the top of its support it undergoes an amazing change. Growth from then is other than by climbing, the leaves are no longer lobed, but elliptic and wavy-edged and it flowers and fruits in spherical bunches 3 to 5cm (1 to 1½in) across. If cuttings are taken from the young growth they will retain the characteristics of it, with lobed leaves and climbing nature. But if cuttings are taken from the top, mature growth, they will retain its characteristics, forming a small bush which flowers and fruits freely. Cuttings of either type are best taken from semi-ripe growth in late summer and planted in pots of sharply-drained compost mixture. Plants are readily available from all the usual sources.

small, pinnate leaves are attractive in themselves, but from June to October are supplemented by 2.5cm (1in)-long tubular orange flowers. Best sown from seed in early spring under glass, the plants are not fully hardy until they are few months old. They can be planted out in May and given some support until they reach their trellis or wires, when they will scramble away happily and, in coastal gardens, remain evergreen. Seed is readily available from garden centres.

Hedera helix Ivy

These hardy, evergreen climbers are ever popular in the garden and as house plants. Extremely tough, they will grow just about anywhere. The young growth, with aerial roots and the classic, three-lobed leaf which is naturally mid to dark green, but now is available in many shades and var-

Hedera helix *Ivy.*

Lathyrus odorata *Sweet pea.*

Lathyrus odorata **Sweet pea**

These lax, grey-green plants with their ovate leaves and tendril-climbing habit, can be annual or perennial; but it is the annuals that have attained massive garden popularity for the showy, long-stemmed flowers, which can be richly scented and will keep coming for almost as long as you keep picking them. Fully hardy, they can be sown from seed in autumn or spring and grown up trellis or canes or allowed to scramble through other plants in the border. They will grow to 2 to 3m (6 to 10ft). Sow in deep pots or toilet-roll tubes and keep well-watered. This needs to be done when they are planted out too, and they are hungry plants, needing a rich soil. But the effort of preparation is worth it if you choose a good variety, of which there are dozens. The spectacular flower show will go on from June to September or later in mild conditions. Transplant only when young, as the roots are deep, and dead-head regularly to prolong flowering. Flowers are available in just about any colour you could wish for.

Lonicera periclymenum *Honeysuckle.*

Lonicera periclymenum **Honeysuckle**

There are many honeysuckles, from all across the northern hemisphere – some climbers and some shrubs, some evergreen and some deciduous – but none can compare with the British and western European native for evening scent. This twining climber twists its stems around whatever support is available, climbing up trees or trellis, through shrubs or pergolas in all kinds of conditions, from sun to shade, and from damp to dry soils, although it takes on its most handsome form if grown in good garden soil and in semi-shade. The distinctive rings of tubular flowers with their prominent stamens can be in shades of yellow, cream, orange or red – or several shades in one flower – and each flower is up to 5cm (2in) long. They are borne in high summer and followed by bunches of bright red berries. The plants will attain a height of from 5 to 6.5m (15 to 20ft) and are deciduous, the leaves turning butter yellow before falling in autumn. Hardwood cuttings are easily rooted in autumn, in sharply drained compost and plants are readily available from all the usual sources.

Mina lobata.

Mina lobata

This dark-leaved relative of the morning glory and bindweed comes from Mexico and is not fully hardy, although it is a perennial in mild climates. The leaves are three-lobed and dark green, setting off the upright racemes of up to twelve 5cm (2in) flowers, that fade through red and yellow to nearly white with age. It prefers full sun but a rich, moist soil. Easily propagated from seed in early spring

and best started under glass and planted out in late spring. Reaches 2 to 3m (6 to 10ft) in height. Climbs by twining and so is good for trellis or to grow through spring-flowering shrubs.

Parthenocissus quinquefolia *Virginia creeper.*

Parthenocissus quinquefolia Virginia creeper

This woody-stemmed, deciduous tendril-climber can reach 15m (50ft) or more if allowed sufficient space. The leaves are made up of five-toothed leaflets, dull green through the summer but turning to glorious shades of crimson in autumn. The insignificant, greenish flowers turn to small, blue-black berries in autumn. Like the honeysuckle, the Virginia creeper will tolerate a significant degree of shade. It grows best in well-drained soil and so will do well against a wall, which it will cover swiftly. Semi-ripe cuttings can be taken in summer or

Solanum crispum *Potato vine.*

hardwood cuttings in early spring and rooted in a mixture of compost and sand. Plants are readily available from garden centres.

Solanum crispum Potato vine

This vigorous, scrambling plant from Chile will attain a height of 5 to 6.5m (15–20ft), with glossy, green, ovate leaves, although there are now garden varieties with variegated leaves. Large bunches of yellow-anthered, mauve flowers up to 1.5cm (¾in) wide are borne from June to September. The plant flowers with spectacular freedom when well grown. It prefers well-drained soil and a warm, sunny position, but will tolerate some shade. Deciduous, it sports bunches of bright, red berries similar to those of the woody nightshade through autumn and into winter. It can be pruned to shape in early spring, before it starts into new growth. Finger-length cuttings of side-shoots can be potted in a sharply drained mixture in summer, then kept warm and moist until rooting is achieved. Plants are readily available from nurseries and garden centres.

Tropaeolum speciosum Climbing nasturtium
Related to the nasturtiums described in Chapter 4 as well as to the canary creeper, which has yellow flowers and palmate leaves, the climbing nasturtium originates from Chile. It is a hardy, perennial, scrambling climber which can achieve 2.5m (10ft) or more, climbing through other shrubs and trees, and is decorated with scarlet flowers from July to September. It prefers some shelter and a rich soil with plenty of water. It will tolerate shade or semi-shade. A good plant for a north-facing spot where little else will grow well.

Tamarix tetranda *Tamarisk.*

Tropaeolum speciosum *Climbing nasturtium.*

There are, of course, many more trees and climbers than those listed above which will suit a coastal garden. They include the following.

Clematis		Many species and varieties for the garden, small-flowered and large, in several colours. Prefers a cool root-run.
Cordyline australis	**Cabbage palm**	Shuttlecock of sword-like leaves. In mild climate will develop stem at the base and grow into a small tree.
Crataegus	**Hawthorn**	Easily pruned as a hedge or left as a tree, with white, pink or cerise flowers in spring and red berries from late summer.
Fraxinus	**Ash**	Medium-sized tree with interesting flowering habit in spring. Deciduous. Divided leaves a little like those of the rowan.
Juniper		Range of sizes and shapes as well as glaucous to light green foliage.
Magnolia		Several types, from small to large, all flowering spectacularly in spring.
Prunus serrula	**Tibetan cherry**	One of many flowering cherries, this has marvellously glossy red bark and a good habit.
Quercus ilex	**Evergreen oak**	A large tree, for those with the space for it.
Salix	**Willow**	Several species and varieties, from small to large. *S. caprea*, the goat willow, is a good choice on the coast.
Solanum dulcamara	**Woody nightshade**	The British native with similar but smaller flowers and glorious berries.
Sorbus aria	**Whitebeam**	Small, highly decorative tree with pale, hairy leaves that turn rich russet in autumn with the red berries.
Trachycarpus fortuneii	**Chusan palm/ Torbay palm**	Dislikes strong winds, but does well in a sheltered coastal garden.
Wisteria floribunda	**Wisteria**	Large and magnificent climber, needs plenty of organic matter dug in at planting time. Not as complicated to prune as some claim.

CHAPTER 8

Garden Maintenance

Having designed, laid out and planted your site, even a low-maintenance garden will need some looking after as time passes. Lawns need to be cut, and may need to be fed, throughout the growing season. Feeding and watering are especially important on the sometimes thin and poor soils of a coastal garden. Flowering plants need to be dead-headed in order to prolong flowering. (It is a good idea to leave a few old flowers on towards the end of the season to allow the collection of seed when it has ripened.) Bushes and trees may need to be pruned to maintain size, shape or productivity and to allow the wind to blow through them. The infamous Leyland cyprus, for example, needs to be kept tightly within the bounds of its required size or it will quickly get out of hand and is then not recoverable since it will not regenerate growth when cut back into old wood.

Of the hard-landscaping elements of the garden, pond pumps will need regular checking, along with the levels of ponds. Wooden structures will need occasional painting or staining. Concrete or other solid paving surfaces will benefit from occasional cleaning. Gravel or chipping paths will need to be weeded every so often. Roofs may collect moss and other debris over time and this must be cleaned off or it will wash down and clog guttering and drain pipes. Especially in the early seasons of a new garden, watering may need to be done regularly. This is more of an issue in coastal gardens than inland sites because of the drying effect of the wind and the salt-laden air. And weeding is an ever-present need for any garden. These are general jobs which can or should be done at any time of the year. However, there are also seasonal chores which help to keep the garden in top condition. Month by month, chores vary from one region to another as well as from one country to another. But, wherever you are, there are jobs to do in any given season.

Even a low-maintenance garden needs some care and attention to continue looking at its best over time. Here both the sage in the foreground and the variegated holly in the background will need regular pruning. There will also need to be done the cleaning of the gravel, dead-heading of the plants and flowering shrubs and the tidying up of the leaves of the bulbs which provide spring colour between the other plants, although they do not feature in this summer photograph.

The choice of plants selected will determine the amount of maintenance required. Here, bedding plants and dahlias have been used for first-year impact. They will need regular watering and feeding, as well as weeding. The shorter dahlias, however, do not need staking as their taller cousins do.

A lower-maintenance option with shrubs, grasses and bulbs planted beneath the gravel mulch.

TOOL CARE

To prolong their life and improve their performance, a little care goes a long way with your garden tools. Spades, trowels, forks and rakes should be cleaned and dried after use. Once a year, in autumn, they should be oiled. A lightweight oil on the metal parts, after sharpening, will prevent the rust which would attack them in the salty seaside atmosphere and a light rub over wooden handles with teak oil or something similar will keep them in good condition also. Mowers and other mechanical tools should also be cleaned after each use. The metal parts should be oiled in autumn and any electrical connections or plugs checked at the same time.

Many consider that the gardening year begins in spring, but there is a lot of activity that goes on through the winter as well. Summer is the season for sitting back and enjoying the garden, but there are jobs to do then too. Autumn is one of the best times of the year for planting, sowing seed and taking cuttings as well as the time of the fruit harvest.

Spring – flowering cherries are in full bloom.

SPRING

This is the time for planting summer bulbs such as gladiolus, lily, crocosmia and freesia. It is also the time to divide and plant the winter bulbs of snowdrop and winter aconite. These, along with cyclamen, are best planted in the green; that is, when they are actively growing, rather than as dry bulbs. If your soil is thin or poor, then these woodland bulbs will benefit from the addition of some compost or other organic matter at this stage.

Hardy perennials can be lifted and divided when they have grown too large and old. Hardy annuals can be sown now in the borders also, filling in around the more permanent planting with a splash of summer colour. Small sowings at regular intervals will provide a longer flowering season, with less need to dead-head. Seedlings sown in the borders in the preceding autumn can now be thinned and those in pots planted out. The growing tips should be pinched out of any which look at all leggy to encourage low, bushy growth. Shrubs, including roses, can be pruned and any new fruit trees are best planted at this time of the year. Existing fruit trees should be treated against fungal diseases such as scab and mildew now, although these are less of a problem on the coast. Dogwoods and decoratively barked willows may be pruned hard at this time to make sure that there is plenty of the new wood that shows its colour best for next autumn and winter. This should be done every three years or so. After pruning, it is a good idea to heel them in again on exposed sites, to deal with any wind-rock that may have occurred over winter.

A slow-release fertilizer can be forked into the ground at this time and new mulch applied. Taller herbaceous perennials should be staked before they get too large. In that way they will grow up through the stakes and hide them, rather than looking trussed later in the season.

Weeding should be started now, hoeing or pulling annual weeds and digging out perennial ones completely. The plants removed in this way should be discarded in the dustbin or burned, not added to the compost heap. This is also the best time of the year to start a new lawn, especially if you are using turf. Existing lawns, having suffered heavy use in the previous year, should be spiked with a garden fork and, on heavy soils, sand should be brushed into the spiking holes to improve drainage. On thin or light soils compost may be used instead. When growth starts, mow lawns with the mower blades set no lower than 2.5cm (1in).

Lawns showing signs of heavy use should be spiked with a fork and have sand brushed in, then a light sowing of seed can be applied and watered in. This is also the time of year to begin sowing annuals for a splash of summer colour in the borders.

Most coastal areas do not suffer unduly from frost. However, if you are in one of those areas where this is not true, then a greenhouse is a useful possession. In it you can now sow tender annuals and perennials and take cuttings from chrysanthemums, fuchsias and dahlias. Greenhouse vegetables may also be sown now, such as tomatoes, peppers and cucumbers.

As pot-grown seedlings come through, they should be thinned to a comfortable distance apart.

Spring is a good time to pick over and clean up decorative mulches such as these, getting them ready for the summer display as the winter weather eases.

PEACHES

Peaches and nectarines blossom early in spring, often so early, in fact, that there are then still few insects around to pollinate them, greatly reducing the potential harvest. This can be easily overcome by the gardener's spending a few minutes with a small paintbrush: simply go around the blossoms, tickling them thoroughly, one by one, with a small, soft brush, thereby transferring pollen from the anthers of one to the stigmas of the next.

Summer hanging baskets may be planted up to fill out, ready for hanging out in three or four weeks' time. Spring-flowering bulbs need to be dead-headed, although the leaves should be left on to feed the bulbs for next year. Bulbs, with their long, narrow leaves designed to reduce transpiration, tend to do well in coastal sites. Actively growing plants in pots, baskets and tubs should be fed regularly and the tips pinched out to promote bushiness.

Summer – fuchsias give a long and brilliant display.

SUMMER

Weeding, watering and dead-heading are the main tasks of the summer, and this is also the main time of the year when pest control is important. Keep a check on plants for any signs of disease or excessive pest attack and treat promptly. Spring-flowering shrubs such as cotoneaster and forsythia can now be pruned, if necessary. Evergreen hedges and shrubs can be clipped, although you should not go back into the brown wood. Suckers should be pulled from roses as soon as they are seen or they will take over and destroy the original hybrid plant.

Fruits must be protected from bird and insect attack as soon as they show the first signs of ripening, if not before. Bushes and strawberry plants may be covered in net, although trees are a more difficult prospect and some losses here are inevitable.

Ponds need more care in summer than at any other time of year. Any excessive plant growth needs to be removed. Pond weed is notorious for growing out of control and must occasionally be raked out. Water levels may need to be topped up in hot spells and the pump needs to be checked regularly and cleaned if necessary.

Lawns need regular mowing, the blade now being lowered to the height required for the finished lawn. They may also be given a weed-and-feed treatment as well as watering in hot weather, where this is permitted. This tends to be especially important in coastal areas, where soils tend to be poorer. However, it should be remembered that drought does not kill a lawn, it simply turns it temporarily brown. Tubs, troughs and hanging baskets, on the other hand, are totally dependent on the gardener for water and so for their survival. They need watering daily now. This is even more important in seaside gardens than in those inland because of the high salt content in the air.

Biennials such as wallflowers, foxgloves and echiums may be sown now, in the borders or in pots for planting out in autumn.

This high-maintenance garden will need a lot of care in summer. There are pots to water, climbers to prune, flowers to dead-head and gravel to keep clean. But a little time each evening or perhaps a blitz every weekend will keep things tidy and at their best.

The pruning of early flowering shrubs and climbers can be done once they have finished flowering. Rambling roses, unlike other types, are best pruned in late summer. Long shoots on wisteria can be cut back to about 30cm (1ft) long. The prunings, when taken deep enough to be classed as semi-ripe, can be used as cuttings to produce more plants. A semi-ripe cutting of a shrub is from the current year's growth and mature enough to be firm, not floppy. Some border perennials, such as carnations and pelargoniums, can now be picked over for cuttings also. Climbers which are still growing well should be trained and tied in as they grow to prevent wind damage. Greenhouses need much ventilation at this time of the year and it is useful to water the floor in the morning and the evening to increase the humidity. Any faded flowers or leaves should be removed immediately to prevent the incursion of diseases such as botritis (grey mould).

Autumn – leaves are changing colour in prelude to falling and fruits are ready for picking.

AUTUMN

The time of harvest, of planting and of sowing, it is also a good season for taking cuttings, as the worst of the heat has gone, reducing the risk of losing prospective new plants to excessive transpiration (water loss through the leaves) while they are trying to establish a new root system.

Autumn is a good time for planting and transplanting shrubs and for giving established ones a final pre-winter trim, to tidy up their shape. Cuttings taken from shrubs and evergreens will root readily. Evergreen shrubs can also be propagated now by the layering method in moist soils.

Shrubs should be heeled in to make sure that they are firmly in the ground before the onset of the winter winds.

Autumn is a good time to look after outside woodwork, before the wet of winter sets in and after the worst of the summer heat is over. Gates, sheds, benches and fences can be cleaned, stained, varnished or oiled as appropriate. Metalwork such as hinges should be brushed down and repainted or oiled now, if they need it.

The seeds of hardy annuals may be sown now, to make sturdy plants for next year, and spring bulbs should be planted – the sooner the better for early flowering varieties such as some of the dwarf narcissi. Herbaceous perennials can be planted in autumn while many of them are in a semi-dormant state and less likely to suffer any stress from the move.

Fruit trees will be ready for harvesting, if it has not already been completed. Apples and pears should not be tugged from the tree but lifted in the hand and twisted gently. If they do not come off easily, then they are not ready. Fallen fruits should be collected and disposed of to prevent the spread of disease. Trees and climbers of all kinds should have their stakes and ties checked, ready for winter, and any that show signs of rocking at the roots should be heeled in firmly. This is a good time to plant new trees too.

There is still time to make a new lawn, by turf or seed, but the existing one should not be given any further feed or weedkiller now. If the surface has been compacted by use, aerate it with a fork after scarifying the lawn to remove dead material, allowing more of the reduced winter light in to the leaves of the grass.

If you have been diligently dead-heading the borders, they will still be in flower and can continue to be dead-headed until the plants are nearly finished. Then you can leave a few flowers to mature and set seed for collection. When the plants are finally finished, clear the beds, fork them over and plant out any spring bedding plants.

Tender plants, such as dahlias, chrysanthemums and gladioli, should be taken in where there is a risk of hard frosts. They may be stored in a frost-free greenhouse or garage over winter and restarted into growth next spring. In milder coastal gardens, however, a mulch over the tops of these plants, after cutting off their tops, may be sufficient to save them for next year.

In the greenhouse, the ventilation will need to be reduced and watering eased off and restricted to mornings to help to prevent the onset of fungal diseases. The greenhouse will need to be cleared out, tidied up and washed down with detergent to further reduce the risk of disease.

The tidying up of outside beds and borders can also be done now, raking up fallen leaves and breaking off dead leaves and stems, although some may

Lavender needs clipping over at the end of summer, but do not cut into the old wood or it will not recover. Lady's mantle will have been dead-headed through the summer and can now be tidied up, ready for winter. Leave fresh leaves on the plant for their decorative effect when wet.

be left on for dramatic effect through the winter. The dead stems of grasses and some hardy annuals and perennials can look striking against the low winter light; the flat, round seed pods of honesty and the spiky foliage and seed heads of sea hollies and globe thistles are prime examples.

Winter – low light through the dead leaves of beech and stems of grasses looks spectacular.

WINTER

Winter in coastal gardens, more than in many others, allows a continuation of the jobs started in autumn: the planting of trees and shrubs, especially bare rooted specimens, the pruning of wisteria and summer-flowering shrubs, and the taking of cuttings for growing on in the greenhouse or coldframe. Take root-cuttings of perennials such as oriental poppies, verbascums, phlox and others. Fork over vacant areas in beds and borders. Prune fruit trees, apart from the *Prunus* genus, and give wisteria a final prune, taking the young shoots back to about 5cm (2in) in length. Check and firm in any plants that may have suffered from wind-rock. If any are actually blown over, then dig them out completely, with as much soil as possible around the roots, and pot them up until you can replant them properly; to try to push them back upright, firm them in and stake them does not work. If a branch of a woody plant is split by the wind and weather, this can be bound tightly back together and the growth beyond it pruned to reduce the risk of further damage. The binding should be checked regularly and removed as soon as the wound has grown back together. This method is effectively the same as grafting. You are simply regrafting the part-broken piece back into place. It will still draw water

Early winter is the time to pay attention to those plants of borderline hardiness. If your garden does not suffer from frost, then simply remove old and tired leaves and the last of any flower heads. Otherwise, this banana would have to be lagged with netting and straw for the winter or brought indoors.

forcing into early growth or flowering. Lawns should be kept clean of leaf debris with a stiff broom. This also levels worm-casts and allows maximum light to reach the grass for strong growth in spring. Keep off the lawn after frost though, since treading on it while it is frozen will damage the leaves.

In late winter you can start the jobs of spring, such as splitting and replanting overgrown clumps of herbaceous perennials and ferns, pruning winter-flowering jasmine and heathers as they fade, and planting the last of the spring-flowering perennials such as primroses and lily-of-the-valley. The

The shrubby honeysuckle in the foreground here will have been pruned in late summer or autumn but the lavatera will benefit from being pruned twice – once in late autumn to prevent wind-rock through the winter and again in late winter, taking it down to two buds from the base to generate fresh, new growth and vigour, ensuring the health and longevity of the plant.

through the section of stem that remained unbroken, as a hedging plant does when it is partly cut through and bent over in the process of hedge-laying.

In the greenhouse growing does not stop and so neither does the work. Watering should be kept to a minimum and done in the mornings. Hardy seeds can be sown and bare-rooted plants put in. Stone fruit also benefit from being sown at this time of year since they generally begin to grow early. Fumigation can prevent or cure pest problems while the summer heat and the length of the day are not exacerbating them. Plants may be brought indoors for dead stems of herbaceous perennials left on over winter for dramatic effect should now be cut down and tidied up. The chrysanthemums and dahlias taken-in last autumn can be started into growth again. The first snowdrops and winter aconites brightening the shady spots of the garden show the promise of a new spring that is about to appear and start the cycle over again.

FROST PROTECTION

Seaside gardens are much less prone to frost than nearby inland locations because the temperature of the sea rarely allows the air above it to freeze. However, if you are using tender plants in temperate climates it is advisable to be aware of the possibility and how to deal with it when a potential problem has been predicted. There are many possible methods, some of which render the plants extremely unattractive for several months and others which require a diligent eye and much work. However, herbaceous plants which die back to ground level in winter can be easily protected with a thick mulch of bark or compost over their crowns. Others, which remain above ground, if not in active growth in the colder seasons, can be sufficiently protected without too much inconvenience. Pot-grown specimens can be taken into a greenhouse, cold frame or shed or moved under a carport. Those in the ground can have a piece of horticultural fleece or bubble-wrap draped over them for the night and pegged down at the corners with canes or something similar when a frost has been forecast.

CHAPTER 9

Pruning and Propagation

PRUNING

Numerous rules and traditions have grown up over the years about pruning, many of which serve only to make it appear much more complicated than it really is. With a few exceptions, most flowering shrubs are best pruned immediately after flowering. This allows for a full appreciation of the flowers while providing the maximum time for the plant to prepare for next year. However, a few plants do not flower on the previous year's growth but on new or even two-year-old wood and a few need pruning at a particular time of year in order to minimize the risk of disease invading the wounds.

Roses are usually pruned in late winter, with a

Camellias are often thought to be difficult to look after and to prune, but this is not true. Given an acid soil and some shelter from frost and strong winds, preferably with a west-facing position, they will thrive and need little pruning. If you do need to prune, do so after flowering, in late May, cutting back to a healthy bud.

light pruning in autumn to help against wind-rock over winter. However, in a coastal garden this double pruning may often be avoided as the conditions are different. The problem of wind-rock in winter is

more significant than the risk of frost, thus a single autumn pruning regime can be adopted. The plants can be taken back hard, to within 15cm (6in) of the ground when they need rejuvenating. This is one of the plant types for which pruning has become an art, but recent research by the British Rose Society has proved that all the fancy techniques are of little purpose. In fact, you can simply take the top foot or so off with a hedge trimmer and have just as good a result as far as flowering is concerned. Nevertheless, it is worthwhile taking out any dead stems right to the base and removing any stems which are rubbing against each other. Thin stems, of insufficient strength to carry blooms, can also be taken off. The exception here is rambling roses, which are pruned in autumn merely to keep them tidy and within the bounds of the required size.

The fruiting currants are pruned in summer and

Some shrubs and trees, such as this hawthorn, oaks, pines and gorse, among others, will be shaped by the wind in exposed situations and any pruning should reflect this tendency.

again in winter. Take out a few of the older branches as soon as you have harvested the fruit and cut back the side shoots by around a third. In winter remove the stems which fruited that year, along with any infected with big-bud mite. The latter should be burned immediately. Gooseberries benefit from a similar regime to the currants.

Apples, pears and cherry trees are best pruned in autumn, when growth has stopped but before the coldest weather causes a reduced disease resistance. The canes of raspberries, loganberries, blackberries and tayberries which have fruited can be cut out after harvest, the remaining growth pruned and the new growth tied in to the supporting wires at this time of year also. Fruit trees and bushes are generally best pruned after cropping, although a light pruning while the fruit is developing will allow a better airflow and so reduce the risk of disease in sheltered sites. Any branches bearing disease that cannot be treated on the plant should be removed and destroyed as soon as the problem is noticed.

Certain climbers have also acquired a mystique around the pruning methods applied to them. Wisteria should be pruned back in midsummer, taking long shoots back to two or three buds. A clematis will be one of two general types – spring flowering or later flowering. The spring flowering ones, such as *C. montana*, can be pruned in summer, simply thinning out as necessary and taking side shoots back to within three buds of the main stems. The rest can be pruned hard back, to within a foot of the ground, in early spring before they begin to green up again after winter dormancy.

Hydrangeas should have the shoots which flow-ered during the summer pruned lightly in the following spring. Never cut back into old wood on a hydrangea or it will be unlikely to recover.

Alpines which flower in spring can be treated as you would the heathers: trim them back with shears after the flowers have finished, to make a neat, bushy plant and prevent straggling. Heathers and lavenders also dislike being pruned back into old wood but benefit from a neatening trim after flowering. The same applies to the brooms and most coniferous shrubs and trees: prune lightly in summer, as often as you need to, to keep them in size, while merely shortening the fresh, green growth. The notable exception to this is yew, which will readily shoot from old wood.

Lavateras benefit from hard pruning in late autumn. Prune them back to within 30 to 45cm (12 to 18in) of the ground, leaving four or five shoots on each stem, as soon as flowering and growth have stopped.

Apart from these few recommendations, any other plants may be pruned as necessary to keep them in shape, both decoratively and in terms of health. Dead or diseased leaves and stems should be removed. Crossing stems which rub against each other should also be taken out to prevent the entry of disease. Pruning should be done a little more harshly in a seaside garden than inland because of the windy conditions and in order to remove some of the salt-contaminated stems and

Bulbs such as these daffodils should not have their leaves pruned – or tidied in any other way – until at least six weeks after flowering is over. This allows the bulbs to build up their strength for flowering next year.

Unlike many shrubs, the evergreen ceanothus can be pruned at any time of year and to whatever degree is felt to be needed. To maintain the maximum impact of flowering, it is best pruned between June and January – after the flowers of the current year and before those of the following year are formed.

leaves. (Salt contamination may also be usefully removed by washing it off periodically with the hose in the early morning or evening, when a harsh sun will not cause scorching.) An attractive shape and plentiful flowering can then be encouraged and cuttings taken for propagation at suitable times of the year.

CUTTINGS

Cuttings count among the chief methods of plant propagation. There are several methods, suitable to different plant types. All need extra care in a sea-side garden, in order to minimize the problem of excessive transpiration. As small a leaf area as possible should be left on the cutting for this reason. Hardwood cuttings are taken in summer or autumn from shrubby plants, including roses.

The cuttings should be from semi-mature wood, rather than the sappy, flexible tips. They may be up to 25cm (10in) long, although shorter if necessary, and should be straight and not branched. Trim the base cleanly with sharp secateurs or a knife, just below a leaf joint, then take the top 4 to 6cm (2 to 3in) off, with a sloping cut just above a leaf joint. All the leaves, except the top two or three, should be removed to reduce transpiration and the base of the cuttings dipped into hormone rooting powder before being pushed into the ground, at least 4cm (1½in) apart, with just the top 4–6cm sticking out. They will slowly root over winter and the following spring.

Softwood cuttings are best taken in spring or summer, but this is not a suitable method for plants with hairy or silver leaves since they may rot off. This method works well for fuchsias and honeysuckles as well as box, privet, lavender, rosemary, weigela, escallonia, cistus, hebe, hibiscus, hydrangeas and bush roses. An 8 to 10cm (3 to 4in) cutting is taken from the non-flowering shoot tip of a suitable plant (if non-flowering tips are unavailable, remove all flowers and buds from cuttings). A cut is made just below a leaf node at the base and all the lower leaves are removed, leaving just a few at the top. Large-leaved plants can benefit from even having these reduced in size. You may safely cut them in half across. Dip the base of the cutting in rooting pow-

der, knock off the excess and then push four or five cuttings into lightly firmed compost in a 4in pot, arranging them around its edge. They should root in about six to eight weeks.

Herbaceous perennials which have several leaves along each stem will also make new plants in this way. Carnations are an easy example: just pull a tip section from a non-flowering shoot, trim off the lower leaves and pop it into a pot of damp compost. Pelargoniums can be propagated in this way also, along with many more similarly structured plants (but it should be noted that pelargoniums do not like rooting powder and that the little, leaf-like projections at each leaf node should be removed with the leaves). Some plants, such as fuchsias, honeysuckle and carnations will even root when a cutting is simply placed in a jar of water. As soon as they have rooted sufficiently, softwood cuttings will start to grow and this is the sign that they require to be potted up individually in order to grow on to usable size.

Sansevierias can be propagated by two methods – division in spring or from leaf-tip cuttings in spring or autumn. Take a leaf tip about 8cm (3in) long and bury the base of it in a sandy compost mix in the greenhouse or on a window sill.

Those herbaceous perennials which do not suit the softwood cutting method may be propagated by either root cuttings or division. The non-clump-forming, hairy or furry-leaved plants, such as verbascums and perennial poppies, take well from root cuttings: 2.5cm (1in)-long sections of pencil-thick root are taken; you can take several from each root, but cut them correctly as you go. It is important to know which way up they go. Make a cut straight across the top of each piece and an angled cut across the bottom, then push it upright into a pot of damp compost, cover it with a plastic bag and wait for the shoots to show. Do not be surprised at having to wait for up to twelve weeks.

Cannas grow from tubers similar to those of dahlias. These can be cut into sections, each with a shoot eye, and potted or planted out individually or the shoots can be allowed to begin growing and then be severed at the junction with the tuber when they are 8 to 10cm (3 to 4in) long, then potted up as cuttings.

DIVISION AND LAYERING

Division is one of the simpler methods of propagation. Clump-forming and some rhizomatous perennials can be dug up and simply split with a sharp blade or a pair of garden forks placed back to back through the clump and forced apart. As long as each section has both roots and shoots, it will grow when replanted. Hardy geraniums are a prime example of the success of this method. Many clump-formers benefit from this treatment every three to five years, keeping them fresh and floriferous. The summer-flowering irises, which grow up from rhizomes, can be lifted and the rhizome (usually an underground stem, although in this case it prefers to bake in full sun on the surface) split into sections, each with some leaf shoots on. The leaves should be cut back to about 15cm (6in) long before each section is replanted.

The final method of vegetative (non-sexual) propagation which deserves a mention here is layering. This is used for those plants from which it is difficult to take cuttings; rhododendrons and magnolias are prime examples. There are two ways of layering a plant – in the ground or in a bag. If it is feasible, the ground method is simpler. Take a low-growing shoot of roughly pencil thickness. Fork plenty of organic matter into the ground beneath it, then cut a trench in this 1in deep. Make a shallow, sloping cut through the bark and into the stem and dust the cut with rooting powder, push the cut down into the trench, peg the branch down and cover it with soil. It can be covered with soil up to about 15cm (6in) from the tip. It may take several months, even a year or more, for the layer to root well, but then the tip will start to grow visibly. This is the sign to expose the cut point and sever the new plant from the old. You may then dig it up and move it to wherever you want.

Bag layering works in exactly the same way but is used when there are no branches low enough for the ground method. The stem is cut and folded in the same way, but, instead of pegging it down to the ground, it is wrapped in a bag full of damp compost – ericaceous in the case of rhododendrons or magnolias – and sealed in with Sellotape or surgical tape. When roots begin to show in the bag you will know that you have been successful and that the new plant can be taken off and potted up.

Magnolia stellata, *along with rhododendrons, camellias and several other trees and shrubs, can be successfully propagated by layering.*

The three different plants in this patio display can be propagated by three different methods. The iresine or blood plant can be propagated by cuttings, placed in a jar of water until they root then potted up in moist compost. The variegated tradescantia can be grown from cuttings in a gritty compost mix, but is more successful by division. And the round-leaved nasturtiums are ridiculously easy from seed, germinating in just a week or so, to be in flower in a few weeks.

SEED

Seed may be sown in pots or direct into the garden, depending on the needs of the plant and the size of the seed itself. Fine, small seed is often best sown in pots or trays for ease of handling and because such seed needs a fine soil and very little covering. Larger, coarser seed can be sown direct into the ground, especially if the plant is of a variety that is hardy where you are.

Pots or trays should be filled with fresh compost to within 1cm (½in) of the top, the surface smoothed off and firmed lightly, then each container placed in water until the top surface of the compost glistens with moisture. Then remove it from the water and sow with seed. Very fine seed may be mixed with a little dry sand so that you can see more easily where you have sown them. Such fine seed will not need to be covered with compost, although larger seeds can benefit from a sprinkling sufficient to cover them. Large seed such as sweet peas can be pushed down 1cm (½in) or so into the compost and covered. A plastic propagator cover or even a sheet of clingfilm can then be put over the pot or tray to prevent it from drying out while you wait for the seed to germinate. A warm environment is often best for this, although there are some notable exceptions, for example, the primulas, most of which like a cool position in which to germinate. A few seed types need special treatment before they will germinate: some need a period of cold, which can be provided by putting them in a refrigerator; some hard-coated seeds benefit from a pre-sowing

Wallflowers grow freely from seed, but flower in the year after sowing, as do most perennials and biennials. They can also be propagated from cuttings. Take semi-ripe stems with no flower buds and break them off with a heel, then plant them in a gritty compost mixture.

soak for a few hours in water; some need heat and some particular elements from smoke. When bought commercially these have usually been pre-treated and so may be sown as normal. Such exceptions to the norm will usually be explained on the seed packets.

Once the seedlings have come through and grown their first two seed leaves, they can be pricked out or potted on. This involves loosening the compost in which they are growing and lifting them out individually by the leaves, not the stem, to be replanted up to the base of the seed leaves with more growing space. They then need a little care while they grow on, keeping the compost moist and the humidity up, by placing them in light shade rather than full sun until they reach 5cm (2in) in height. They can then be brought out into the light and their tips pinched out to encourage branching and bushiness. Another inch or so of height and they can finally be planted out into their flowering positions, perhaps with another pinching out of the growing tips, both at the tops and on the

PROPAGATORS

With or without a greenhouse, if you intend to grow plants from seed you may find a propagator useful. Some seeds require a warm environment in which to germinate and the propagator is the most efficient way for the gardener to provide this. Powered either by paraffin or electricity, they perform the twin functions of providing bottom heat and a clear cover to prevent evaporation.

branches of the little plants to make them bushier still and to allow maximum flowering potential. There are few things as satisfying as propagating your own plants, especially from seed, and there is no reason why everyone cannot do it. A 2m (6ft)-square greenhouse can easily produce a thousand young plants in a year and even a window sill can be used with surprising results. A little work can go a long way towards giving you a great sense of pride in your garden.

Just a few packets of seed, a bag of compost, a little water and care is all you need to produce a garden full of colour in just a few short weeks with annuals such as these.